Focus on
LITERACY

Teacher's Resource Book 5

Barry and Anita Scholes

Authors: Barry and Anita Scholes

Design: Grasshopper Design Company; Amanda Easter

Editor: Jock Graham

Cover image: Dan Gair, Tony Stone Images

Illustrations: Pat Murray

Published by Collins Educational
An imprint of HarperCollins*Publishers* Ltd
77–85 Fulham Palace Road
Hammersmith
London W6 8JB

Telephone ordering and information:
0870 0100 441

The HarperCollins website address is:
www.**fire**and**water**.com

First published 1999
Reprinted 1999, 2000

ISBN 0 00 302521 7

British Library Cataloguing in Publication Data
A catalogue record for this book is available from the British Library.

Printed in Great Britain by Martins the Printers, Berwick-upon-Tweed

Contents

Focus on Literacy and the National Literacy Strategy

You will find in *Focus on Literacy* a strong support in the teaching of reading and writing within the context of a literacy hour. All the literacy objectives of the National Literacy Strategy for each term may be covered by using the Big Book anthologies together with the Pupil's Book, the Homework Book, the Copymasters and the Teacher's Resource Book. Here, in one grand design, are sufficient teaching materials for five full literacy hours per week throughout the entire school year.

The aims of *Focus on Literacy*

The aims of *Focus on Literacy* are identical to those of the National Literacy Strategy: to develop each child's ability to read and write. It promotes their development by honing the literary skills necessary to meet the Range, Key Skills, and Standard English and Language Study of the National Curriculum Programmes of Study.

These skills are wide-ranging and specific, and worthy of review:

- to read and write with confidence, fluency and understanding
- to use a full range of reading cues (phonic, graphic, syntactic, contextual) to self-monitor their reading and correct their own mistakes
- to understand the sound and spelling system and use this to read and spell accurately
- to acquire fluent and legible handwriting
- to have an interest in words and word meanings, and to increase vocabulary
- to know, understand and be able to write in a range of genres in fiction and poetry, and understand and be familiar with some of the ways that narratives are structured through basic literary ideas of setting, character and plot
- to understand and be able to use a range of non-fiction texts
- to plan, draft, revise and edit their own writing
- to have a suitable technical vocabulary through which they can understand and discuss their reading and writing
- to be interested in books, read with enjoyment and evaluate and justify preferences
- to develop their powers of imagination, inventiveness and critical awareness through reading and writing.

The NLS framework and *Focus on Literacy*

The NLS teaching objectives for reading and writing are set out in termly units to ensure progression. Each term's work focuses on specific reading genres and related writing activities. *Focus on Literacy* offers carefully selected examples of these reading genres and stimulating activities relating to them.

The overall structure is the same for each term and is divided into three strands: text, sentence and word levels. Text level refers to comprehension and composition, sentence level to grammar and punctuation, and word level to phonics, spelling and vocabulary. The activities in *Focus on Literacy* offer many opportunities for the development of handwriting, while leaving you free to follow your school's own writing policy.

The Literacy Hour and *Focus on Literacy*

The NLS framework requires a literacy hour as part of school work each day. The literacy hour is designed to establish a common pattern for all classes and is carefully structured to ensure a balance between whole class and group teaching, as the diagram below shows.

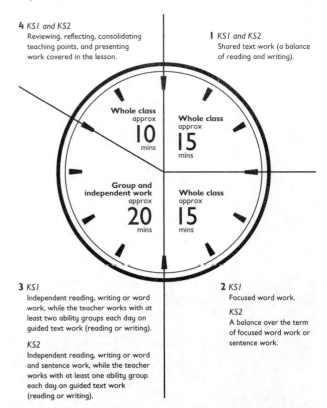

4 *KS1 and KS2*
Reviewing, reflecting, consolidating teaching points, and presenting work covered in the lesson.

1 *KS1 and KS2*
Shared text work (a balance of reading and writing).

Whole class approx **10** mins

Whole class approx **15** mins

Group and independent work approx **20** mins

Whole class approx **15** mins

3 *KS1*
Independent reading, writing or word work, while the teacher works with at least two ability groups each day on guided text work (reading or writing).

KS2
Independent reading, writing or word and sentence work, while the teacher works with at least one ability group each day on guided text work (reading or writing).

2 *KS1*
Focused word work.

KS2
A balance over the term of focused word work or sentence work.

This structure enables you to spend up to 100 per cent of your time in direct teaching. Children work in a direct teaching relationship for approximately 60 per cent of the time and independently for the remaining 40 per cent.

The high-quality texts of *Focus on Literacy* and the related activities directly meet the NLS objectives, and so relieve you of the burden of deciding *what* to teach. The teacher's notes support you in planning *how* to use the materials in your teaching.

Shared whole class time

Shared whole class time takes place during the first half of the literacy hour. It is divided into 15 minutes of shared text work (a balance of reading and writing) and 15 minutes of focused word and sentence work. This is the time when you can effectively model the reading/writing process with the children.

In shared reading you can help to extend reading skills in line with the NLS objectives, teaching and reinforcing grammar, punctuation and vocabulary.

The reading texts also provide ideas and structures for shared writing. Working with the whole class, you create the opportunity to teach grammar and spelling skills, to demonstrate features of layout and presentation, and to focus on editing and refining work. The shared writing will also be the starting point for independent writing.

Independent activities

The shared whole class time of the literacy hour is followed by 20 minutes of independent activities. During this time you will probably work with a guided reading or writing group, while the children will be working independently, but within a group organised by ability to cater for differentiation.

To help you with this, the word and sentence work in the Pupil's Book is divided into two, three or four sections identified as A, B, C and D; A is the easiest and D is the hardest. It is important to match carefully these activities to the children's ability, and to explain them thoroughly before the children begin. This leaves you free to work with your group without interruptions from children seeking your further support.

Each section is short so that children will be able to complete the activities you select in the time available. The Homework Book is available for those who finish early and wish to keep busy, as well as for work outside the classroom. Other activities which the children may do during this time are independent reading and preparing presentations for the class.

It is suggested that you aim to work with each guided reading and writing group for two sessions per week, organised so that you see each child in the class at least once.

Plenary

The final 10 minutes of the literacy hour is a plenary session for reviewing, reflecting upon and consolidating teaching points, and presenting work covered in the lesson. This is an essential element of the hour. It is important to plan this activity so that every child has the opportunity to feed back once as part of their group during the course of a week. A different objective will be featured each day so that each objective is reinforced in turn. This will allow you to monitor each group's progress and highlight the teaching/learning points as necessary.

Using *Focus on Literacy*

The Big Book anthologies

There are three Big Book anthologies, each covering a term's work. These consist of carefully chosen texts for shared work on word, sentence and text levels. The extracts also provide the context for the independent activities. Each unit provides texts for a week's shared reading.

Each extract in the anthology begins with a short introduction, placing the text that follows in context. The extract is accompanied by a *To think and talk about* section to prompt and stimulate the children's responses.

Further teaching points and suggestions are given in the Teacher's Resource Book.

The Pupil's Book

The Pupil's Book is made up of 30 units. Each unit begins with the main text and is followed by the independent activities for the week.

To help you with differentiation, the independent activities are identified for level of difficulty, section A being the easiest and D the hardest. Each section is scaled to a workable size. By matching the level of difficulty to a group's ability level, you can help assure that children can complete the activities in the time available.

The five-day spread

The independent activity for **Day 1** is text-based. Section A has questions for literal recall, while those in section B are inferential. These independent questions are in addition to those in the *To think and talk about* section, which are intended as shared reading questions in order for you to help the children to explore the text in greater depth.

Day 2 independent activities focus on word, sentence or text work.

Day 3 begins with shared writing, followed by independent writing.

Day 4 is the same as Day 3.

Day 5 completes the word, sentence or text work.

'Stickers' provide the children with the facts they need to complete the work and make the most of the activities.

The Homework Book

The Homework Book contains activities which consolidate and extend the work in the Pupil's Book.

This book is equally useful in the classroom outside the literacy hour and out of the classroom for work at home.

The Teacher's Resource Book

The Teacher's Resource Book comprises notes, copymasters, assessment masters, record sheets and NLS charts. It also outlines a basic approach to each unit in the Big Books and Pupil's Book and includes two award certificates.

The teacher's notes and you

The teacher's notes help you use the *Focus on Literacy* material to the best advantage. The notes are arranged in five sections, each covering one literacy hour. These are further subdivided according to the literacy format: shared text/shared writing work, focused word/sentence work, independent work, and plenary.

A termly planning chart introduces each group of ten units. This chart lists the range of texts for that term, the word, sentence and text work which is explicitly covered, and the continuous work which will be part of your teaching throughout the term, such as practising reading and spelling strategies.

The teacher's notes for each text are organised to facilitate the literacy hour.

A *Key Learning Objectives* box lists the key literacy objectives covered in that week's work, and a *Resources* box identifies the range of texts covered, details of the extracts, and the page references of all the components used in the unit.

Details are given of any special preparation you need to do for the unit, for example providing dictionaries.

The *Shared reading* section lists teaching points and suggestions on how to explore the meaning of the text, in line with the literacy framework objectives. In fiction and poetry this entails exploring genres, settings, characters, plots, themes, figurative language, authorship and the way different texts are organised. In non-fiction texts this involves genres, structures and presentation, identifying main points, skimming and scanning, following an argument, exploring steps in a process, comparing different sources and differentiating fact, opinion and persuasion.

The texts often provide both structure and content for writing activities, and the context for many of the activities at sentence and word level on the copymasters.

The *Shared writing* section offers guidance on how texts are composed. The main text studied in earlier shared reading sessions will provide the ideas and structure for this writing. Each shared writing activity is the starting point for subsequent independent writing.

The *Focused word/sentence work* section offers appropriate teaching points and suggestions for investigating text in detail to explore how its message is influenced by style: language, grammar, choice of vocabulary and presentation. The Pupil's Book supports independent consolidation of the work.

The *Independent work* section introduces the independent reading, writing or word and sentence activities which may be found in the Pupil's Book, the Homework Book or on Copymasters.

The *Plenary* section has suggestions for reviewing and reflecting upon the work covered, consolidating teaching points and presenting work.

A *Consolidation and extension* section has ideas and suggestions for follow-up activities.

The *Homework* section describes the related activity in the Homework Book.

Copymasters

The Copymasters offer a range of support material among which are book reviews, planning sheets, charts for collecting and classifying words, and consolidation and extension work.

Assessment

To facilitate assessment there is an assessment master for each term, and a self-assessment master for the year's work.

Record keeping

Record sheets are provided at the back of the Teacher's Resource Book. They feature a summary of the term's objectives, each with a space for your comments.

Award certificates

Photocopiable award certificates are provided to reward significant individual achievements in literacy.

NLS charts

A chart listing all literacy objectives for the year, and showing how these are covered by *Focus on Literacy* materials, is included in the back of the Teacher's Resource Book.

Basic approach to each unit

The basic approach to each unit in *Focus on Literacy* is as follows:

Day 1

Shared **reading** of the week's main text in the Big Book.

Focused word/sentence work based on the main text.

Independent text work on the main text, which is reproduced in the Pupil's Book.

Plenary session for which there are suggestions in the teacher's notes.

Day 2

Further shared **reading** of the main text.

Further focused word/sentence work based on the main text.

Independent word, sentence or text work in the Pupil's Book.

Plenary suggestions in the teacher's notes.

Day 3

Shared **writing**, using the main text as a model or stimulus.

Focused word/sentence work, appropriate to the shared writing task.

Independent writing, using guidance in the Pupil's Book.

Plenary suggestions in the teacher's notes.

Day 4

Shared **reading** of the second text in the Big Book.

Focused word/sentence work based on the second text.

Continuation of the independent writing from Day 3.

Plenary suggestions in the teacher's notes.

Day 5

Further shared **reading** of the second text.

Focused word/sentence work based on the second text.

Independent word, sentence or text work in the Pupil's Book.

Plenary suggestions in the teacher's notes.

This approach is flexible, occasionally varied to make the most of the week's activities. For example, the shared reading for Day 4 might be replaced by shared writing when more extended written work is being developed; shared writing might begin on Day 2; or the second text might be shared on Day 2.

Work outside the literacy hour

The Copymasters and Homework Book provide activities for outside the literacy hour and outside the classroom.

The extracts in *Focus on Literacy* are only part of the genre coverage. You will need time outside of the literacy hour to read aloud to your class, giving children the opportunity to hear complete stories, novels and poems. You will also need to show them complete non-fiction texts, so that features such as covers, blurbs, information about authors, contents, indexes and chapter headings can be discussed and appreciated. Children will need further time for their own independent reading for interest and pleasure, and older pupils will need time for extended writing.

You can help to reinforce genre features when children choose books for independent reading, or during guided reading sessions when you are working with a group.

Big Book contents

BIG BOOK 5B   TERM 2

BIG BOOK 5C   TERM 3

THE COURSE COMPONENTS
Pupil's Book contents

TERM 1

TERM 2

TERM 3

Homework Book contents

TERM 1

TERM 2

TERM 3

Copymaster checklist

TERM 1

Unit 1	1	Story openings
	2	Investigating character
	3	Reading log
Unit 2	4	Book review
	5	How stories are structured
	6	Collecting everyday expressions
Unit 3	7	Comparing poems by the same author
Unit 4	8, 9	Glossary of language terms
	10	How a story develops
Unit 6	11	Anne Frank's Diary
Unit 8	12	Story board
Unit 9	13	Books with lasting appeal
Unit 10	14	Revision – term 1 assessment master

TERM 2

Unit 12	15	Different versions of the same story
Unit 14	16	Finding out: planning sheet
	17	Finding out: finding and recording information
Unit 16	18	Exploring genre
Unit 17	19	A glossary of terms
	20	Comparing information texts
Unit 20	21	Book review
	22	Revision – term 2 assessment master

TERM 3

Unit 21	23	Reading journal
	24	Words borrowed from other languages
Unit 25	25	Persuasive words and phrases
Unit 27	26	Finding out
Unit 28	27	Exploring dialect words
Unit 30	28	How am I getting on? – self-assessment
	29	Revision – 1: term 3 assessment master
	30	Revision – 2: Y5 assessment master

Teacher's Notes

Year 5 • Terms 1–3

SCHOOL _____   CLASS _____   TEACHER _____

		Phonetics, spelling and vocabulary	Grammar and punctuation	Comprehension and composition	Texts
Continuous work Weeks I–5		WL 1, 2, 3	SL 2, 3, 6, 8		**Range** Fiction and poetry: novels, stories and poems by significant children's writers; playscripts; concrete poetry
Blocked work **Week**	**Unit**				**Titles**
I	I		SL 2, 5, 7	TL 1, 3, 4, 9, 10, 12, 13, 15	From *Harry's Mad*, Dick King-Smith; From *Babe (The Sheep-Pig)*, Dick King-Smith
2	2	WL 4, 5, 9	SL 3	TL 1, 2, 8, 9, 10, 12, 15	From *Time Trouble* and *A Stitch in Time*, Penelope Lively
3	3	WL 5	SL 5	TL 6, 7, 8, 16	*Rodge Said*, Michael Rosen; *The Silver Fish*, Shel Silverstein; *W*, James Reeves; *League Division Fun*, Michael Rosen; *Ping-Pong*, Eve Merriam; *Giant Rocket*, Wes Magee; *Waves*, Jerome Fletcher; untitled shape poem on the neck of a giraffe, Shel Silverstein
4	4	WL 7, 10	SL 7	TL 5, 12, 14, 18, 19, 20	From *Roald Dahl's The BFG – plays for children*, adapted by David Wood; From *The BFG*, Roald Dahl
5	5	WL 6	SL 8	TL 1, 3, 5, 8, 18, 19, 20	From *The Phantom Sausage Stealer*, Johnny Ball

Focus on Literacy Teacher's Resource Book 5 © Barry and Anita Scholes, HarperCollins*Publishers* Ltd 1999

TERM 1

HALF TERMLY PLANNER

Year 5 • Term 1 • Weeks 6–10

SCHOOL _____   CLASS _____   TEACHER _____

	Phonetics, spelling and vocabulary	Grammar and punctuation	Comprehension and composition	Texts
Continuous work **Weeks 6–10**	WL 1, 2, 3	SL 2, 3, 6, 8		**Range** **Fiction and poetry**: novels, stories and poems by significant children's writers **Non-fiction**: recounts of events, activities, observational records, news reports; instructional texts: rules, instructions
Blocked work **Week / Unit**				**Titles**
6 / 6	WL 8		TL 4, 9, 21, 24, 26	From *The Diary of Anne Frank*; *United's cup hopes dashed*
7 / 7		SL 3, 9	TL 22, 23, 25, 26, 27	From *Liquid Magic*, Philip Watson; *Growing Seeds*
8 / 8		SL 2, 4, 6, 8	TL 3, 4, 9, 23, 26, 27	From *The Dancing Bear* and *Tom's Sausage Lion*, Michael Morpurgo
9 / 9		SL 1, 6	TL 1, 3, 11, 12	From *The Railway Children*, E. Nesbit; From *The Secret Garden*, Frances Hodgson Burnett
10 / 10	WL 7	SL 6	TL 7, 16, 17	*Ant*, Zoe Bailey; *What is ... the Sun?*, Wes Magee; *What is fog?*, John Foster; from *Paper Boats*, Rabindranath Tagore; *At Kisagata*, Matsuo Basho; *At the butterflies*, Issa; *Steel Band Jump Up*, Faustin Charles

Dick King-Smith

Key Learning Objectives

TL1 To analyse the features of a good opening and compare story openings

TL3 To investigate how characters are presented, referring to the text:
– through dialogue, action and description
– how the reader responds to them

TL4 To consider how texts can be rooted in the writer's experience

TL9 To develop an active attitude towards reading: seeking answers, anticipating events, empathising with characters and imagining events that are described

TL10 To evaluate a book by referring to details and examples in the text

TL12 To discuss the enduring appeal of established authors

TL13 To record their ideas, reflections and predictions about a book through a reading log or journal

TL15 To write new scenes or characters into a story, in the manner of the writer, maintaining consistency of character and style, using paragraphs to organise and develop detail

SL2 To understand the basic conventions of standard English and consider when and why standard English is used:
– agreement between nouns and verbs
– avoidance of non-standard dialect words

SL5 To understand the difference between direct and reported speech through:
– finding and comparing examples from reading
– transforming direct into reported speech and vice versa, noting changes in punctuation and words that have to be changed or added

SL7 From reading, to understand how dialogue is set out, e.g. on separate lines for alternate speakers in narrative, and the positioning of commas before speech marks

Range	Novels by significant children's writers
Texts:	From *Harry's Mad*, Dick King-Smith From *Babe* (*The Sheep-Pig*), Dick King-Smith
Resources:	Big Book 5A pp 4–7 Pupil's Book 5 pp. 2–4 Homework Book 5 p. 2: Direct and reported speech Copymaster 1: Story openings Copymaster 2: Investigating character Copymaster 3: Reading log

Preparation

• If possible, make available a selection of books by Dick King-Smith for the children to read, enjoy and discuss.

DAY 1

Big Book 5A pp. 4–5; Pupil's Book pp. 2–3

Shared reading

• Do the children think this is a good opening to the story? What makes them think so? Does it make them want to read on? How important do they think a good opening is to a story?

• How is Harry introduced to the reader: through dialogue, action or description? What are we told about him?

Focused word/sentence work

• Revise verb tense. Ask the children to identify present and past tense verbs. Experiment with transforming one tense into another.

• Investigate the use of punctuation marks in the text: exclamation marks, dashes, commas, speech marks, brackets, the apostrophe, capital letters.

Independent work

• Children answer questions on the text. The questions are organised into three sections. Section A questions draw literal evidence from the text and are multiple-choice. Section B questions are inferential and require one or two sentence answers, while section C has a single question requiring a longer answer, responding to the text as a whole. This structure offers opportunities for differentiation while at the same time preparing for SATs.

Plenary

• Review the children's independent text work. Explain how to use the text to find literal answers, and how to use clues where information is not given directly.

DAY 2

Big Book 5A pp. 4–5; Pupil's Book p. 3

Shared reading

• Ask the children to explain fully what Harry was trying to do that morning.

• What do the children think of his behaviour? Why does he behave in that way? How might it be dangerous?

• Ask the children to explain fully what went wrong that morning.

• Suppose he had come down the stairs in the normal way. Would this have made the opening more, or less, interesting? Why?

Focused word/sentence work

• Which are the spoken words in the passage? What special punctuation marks indicate these words?

• Discuss the use of speech marks and other associated punctuation, e.g. commas, capital letters.

• Investigate writing spoken words as direct speech.

Independent work

• Children consolidate their understanding of direct speech.

Plenary

- Review the children's independent work on direct speech, re-emphasising teaching points and clarifying misconceptions.

DAY 3

Big Book 5A pp. 4–5; Pupil's Book p. 4

Shared reading and writing

- Read the opening to *Harry's Mad* again. Discuss how the story might continue. What has happened to Harry? What has happened to his mother? Where is his father? What will his parents say and do next? Why is the postman ringing the bell?
- Use the notes in the Pupil's Book to plan a continuation of the story.
- Write the first paragraph together in the manner of Dick King-Smith. Aim for consistency of character and style.

Focused word/sentence work

- Revise how direct speech is set out. Incorporate dialogue into the shared writing.

Independent work

- Children begin their continuation of the story of Harry Holdsworth.

Plenary

- Review the work in progress. Encourage the children to discuss, proofread and edit their own writing for clarity and correctness.

DAY 4

Big Book 5A pp. 6–7; Pupil's Book p. 4

Shared reading

- Dick King-Smith worked as a farmer and a teacher before becoming one of our most popular children's writers. Which of these experiences is he using in the extract from *Babe* (originally published as *The Sheep-Pig*)?
- How does the story open: with dialogue, action or description?
- Do the children think this is a good opening to the story? What makes them think so? Does it make them want to read on?
- How are the characters introduced to us: through dialogue, action or description?

Focused word/sentence work

- Discuss the use of non-standard English in the dialogue: non-standard dialect words ("theseyer cakes") and non-agreement between nouns and verbs ("afore you does").
- Why does the writer use these non-standard English phrases? Why do they only appear in the dialogue? What do they tell us about Mrs Hogget?

Independent work

- Children continue their story about Harry Holdsworth.

Plenary

- Review the children's writing in an atmosphere of constructive criticism. Discuss how successful they have been in writing in the manner of the original, maintaining consistency in character and style.
- Encourage the children to discuss, proofread and edit their own writing for clarity and correctness.

DAY 5

Big Book 5A pp. 6–7; Pupil's Book p. 4

Shared reading

- What do the children think the strange noise is? What clues are there in the text?
- Do they think Farmer Hogget knows what it is? What makes them think so?
- Compare the opening of this story to that of *Harry's Mad*. In what ways is it similar or different?
- Discuss reasons why Dick King-Smith is one of our most popular authors.

Focused word/sentence work

- Investigate how the dialogue is set out as direct speech: with speech marks, commas before speech marks, and separate lines for alternate speakers.
- Explain how to change direct speech into reported speech, noting the changes in punctuation and words that have to be changed or added. Notice that statements in direct speech can usually be changed to reported speech by beginning with the words, *X said that ...* Reported speech questions usually begin *X asked if ...* or *X asked when, where, why, how, who*, etc. Other changes are: *I* and *we* change to *he*, *she* or *they* unless the writer is writing about himself; present tense changes to past tense.

Independent work

- Children practise transforming direct speech into reported speech and vice versa.

Plenary

- Review the week's work, consolidating teaching points.

Consolidation and extension

- Collect examples of reported speech from reading.
- Copymaster 1 is a book review focusing on story openings, encouraging the children to analyse the opening of a book and to compare it to another book they have read.
- Copymaster 2 is a book review sheet structured to help the children to respond to a character by considering how that character is introduced, how he or she behaves and the nature of his/her relationship with other characters in the book.
- Copymaster 3 may be used as a reading log. Encourage the children to make notes of their ideas, reflections and predictions about a book *as they read it*.

Homework

- Page 2 in the Homework Book consolidates work on direct and reported speech.

Unit 2 Penelope Lively

Key Learning Objectives

TL1	To analyse the features of a good opening and compare a number of story openings
TL2	To compare the structure of different stories, to discover how they differ in pace, build-up, sequence, complication and resolution
TL8	To investigate and collect different examples of wordplay, relating form to meaning
TL9	To develop an active attitude towards reading: seeking answers, anticipating events, empathising with characters and imagining events that are described
TL10	To evaluate a book by referring to details and examples in the text
TL12	To discuss the enduring appeal of established authors
TL15	To write new scenes into a story, in the manner of the writer, maintaining consistency of character and style, using paragraphs to organise and develop detail
SL3	To discuss, proofread and edit their own writing for clarity and correctness, e.g. by creating more complex sentences, using a range of connectives, simplifying clumsy constructions
WL4	To examine the properties of words ending in vowels other than the letter *e*
WL5	To investigate, collect and classify spelling patterns in pluralisation: adding *s* and *es*
WL9	To collect and classify a range of idiomatic phrases, clichés and expressions. To compare, discuss and speculate about meaning/origins and check in dictionaries; use in own writing and be aware of when it is appropriate to use these in speech and writing

Range:	Novels and stories by significant children's writers
Texts:	From *Time Trouble* and *A Stitch in Time*, Penelope Lively
Resources:	Big Book 5A pp. 8–10 Pupil's Book 5 pp. 5–7 Homework Book 5 p. 3: Plurals Copymaster 4: Book review Copymaster 5: How stories are structured Copymaster 6: Collecting everyday expressions

Preparation

- If possible, make available a selection of children's books by Penelope Lively for the children to read, enjoy and discuss.
- Make available *Brewer's Dictionary of Phrase and Fable* to investigate the origins of everyday expressions.

DAY 1

Big Book 5A pp. 8–9; Pupil's Book pp. 5–6

Shared reading

- How does *Time Trouble* open: with dialogue, action or description?
- Do the children think this is a good story opening? Ask them to give reasons for their answers. Compare this opening with those in Unit 1.
- What kind of person do the children think the storyteller is? What makes them think so?

Focused word/sentence work

- Ask the children to identify the use of dialogue in the text. Investigate how it is presented.
- Experiment with using adverbs to qualify verbs in the dialogue, e.g. "I'd give anything to have this afternoon all over again," said the storyteller *angrily, loudly, softly, sadly*.

Independent work

- Children answer questions on the text.

Plenary

- Review the children's independent text work. Explain how to use the text to find literal answers, and how to use clues where information is not given directly. Make sure they understand the need to answer section C as fully as possible.

DAY 2

Big Book 5A pp. 8–9; Pupil's Book p. 6

Shared reading

- Improvise the bad afternoon the storyteller had with his brother, mother and teachers.
- What do the children think will happen next in the story? What makes them think so?

Focused word/sentence work

- Investigate the everyday expressions in the story, e.g. *killing time, spending time, summer time, half-time, the time of your life*.
- Discuss other everyday expressions, e.g. *under the weather, taken for a ride, put on a brave face, putting his back up*.

Independent work

- Children investigate everyday expressions.

Plenary

- Review the children's independent work. Use *Brewer's Dictionary of Phrase and Fable* to investigate the origins of the expressions.

DAY 3

Big Book 5A pp. 8–9; Pupil's Book p. 7

Shared reading and writing

- Read *Time Trouble* again, with a view to continuing the story in a similar style. Note that the opening tells us that the arrangement with the grandfather clock proved disastrous.
- Brainstorm ideas for the plot and make notes.
- Select the best ideas and discuss how to organise them into paragraphs.
- Tell the children that they will be expected to revise and proofread their work.

Focused word/sentence work

- Revise how to set out direct speech.

Independent work

- Children begin writing a continuation of the story.

Plenary

- Review the work in progress. Encourage those who have finished a first draft to check and improve their work.

DAY 4

Big Book 5A p. 10; Pupil's Book p. 7

Shared reading

- Read the extract from *A Stitch in Time*.
- Discuss the detail which builds up a picture of the rainy day. Which words and phrases do the children think describe the rain best?
- What does the passage tell us about Maria?
- Encourage the children to imagine they are Maria. How do they think she feels?

Focused word/sentence work

- Investigate ways of adapting the first paragraph for a younger reader, by changing its length, vocabulary, tone and sentence structures.

Independent work

- Children complete their stories, and edit and proofread their work.

Plenary

- Ask some children to read their stories aloud. Evaluate their writing in an atmosphere of constructive criticism.

DAY 5

Big Book 5A p. 10; Pupil's Book p. 7

Shared reading

- Ask the children to read the text aloud, using punctuation as an aid to reading.
- Compare this story with the extract from *Time Trouble*. What similarities and differences are there?

Focused word/sentence work

- Look at the word "roof" in the text. How is it made plural? What is the basic rule for making words plural? What is the plural of *bush*? What is the spelling rule for words ending in *ch*, *sh*, *s* or *x*? If the children are unable to construct a rule, give them examples of such plurals, e.g. *buses, bushes, boxes, matches*.
- What is the general rule for pluralising words ending in *o*? Ask the children for exceptions to this rule, e.g. *radios, pianos, solos*.

Independent work

- Children consolidate their understanding of making plurals by adding *s* and *es*.

Plenary

- Review the week's work, re-emphasising teaching points and clarifying misconceptions.

Consolidation and extension

- Copymaster 4 is a book review which encourages the children to evaluate a book by referring to details and examples in the text.
- Copymaster 5 helps children to analyse how stories are structured, and enables them to compare the structure of different stories.
- Copymaster 6 encourages the children to collect everyday expressions and to record what they mean.
- Use *Brewer's Dictionary of Phrase and Fable* to investigate the origins of everyday expressions.
- Read other books by Penelope Lively, or another author the children know well. Use Copymaster 5 to help the children compare how they differ in pace, build-up, complication and resolution.

Homework

- Page 3 in the Homework Book consolidates understanding of forming plurals using *s* and *es*.

23

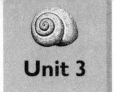

Unit 3 — Funny Verse

Key Learning Objectives

TL6	To read a number of poems by significant poets and identify what is distinctive about the style or content of their poems
TL7	To analyse and compare poetic style, use of forms and the themes of significant poets; to respond to shades of meaning; to explain and justify personal tastes; to consider the impact of full rhymes, half rhymes, internal rhymes and other sound patterns
TL8	To investigate and collect different examples of wordplay, relating form to meaning
TL16	To convey feelings, reflections or moods in a poem through the careful choice of words and phrases
SL5	To understand the difference between direct and reported speech: – transforming direct into reported speech and vice versa, noting changes in punctuation and words that have to be changed or added
WL5	To investigate, collect and classify spelling patterns in pluralisation, construct rules from regular spellings: change *f* to *ves*; when *y* is preceded by a consonant, change to *ies*; when *y* is preceded by a vowel, add *s*

Range:	Poems by significant children's writers; concrete poems
Texts:	*The Silver Fish*, and an untitled shape poem on the neck of a giraffe, Shel Silverstein; *W*, James Reeves; *League Division Fun* and *Rodge Said*, Michael Rosen; *Ping-Pong*, Eve Merriam; *Waves*, Jerome Fletcher; *Giant Rocket*, Wes Magee
Resources:	Big Book 5A pp. 11–15 Pupil's Book 5 pp. 8–11 Homework Book 5 p. 4: More plurals: words ending in *f* and *y* Copymaster 7: Comparing poems by the same author

Preparation

• If possible, collect other poems by the poets who are featured in this unit. Use these for comparison of content and style, in either shared reading sessions or independently, using Copymaster 7.

• Note that writing poems constitutes the activities for days 3, 4 and 5.

Big Book 5A pp. 11–13; Pupil's Book pp. 8–9

Shared reading

• Read and enjoy the poems.

• In what ways are the poems similar? How are they different?

• Which poems play with words?

• Investigate *League Division Fun* line by line, examining the wordplay. Which examples rely on homophones? (e.g. *won/one*; *Leeds/leads*; *ate/eight*; *too/two*).

• Explore the rhythm of *Ping-Pong*. What does it remind the children of? Why does the last line end with a word of one syllable? Investigate how the double words have been selected to rhyme. Is the rhyming pattern regular?

• Which of the two poems do the children like best? Why?

Focused word/sentence work

• Ask the children to suggest more double words, e.g. *tick tock*, *splish splash*, *hurly burly*. Make a list. Discuss their meanings. Keep the list for use on days 3, 4 and 5.

Independent work

• Children answer questions on the poems.

Plenary

• Review the children's independent text work.

Big Book 5A pp. 11–13; Pupil's Book p. 9

Shared reading

• Ask the children to explain the humour in the poems.

• The humour in *W* relies on rhyme for its effect, as to some extent does *The Silver Fish*. Discuss the differences between half rhymes (*fishes/delicious*), full rhymes (*wishes/fishes*) and double rhymes (*double you/trouble you*).

• In what ways is *Rodge Said* different from the other two poems? (It describes something that may have really happened.)

• Which of these poems do the children like best? Why?

Focused word/sentence work

• Investigate the use of direct speech in the poems.

• Experiment with changing the direct speech into reported speech.

Independent work

• Children consolidate their understanding of changing direct to reported speech and vice versa.

Plenary

• Review the children's independent work. Consolidate teaching points, clarifying any misconceptions.

DAY 3

Big Book 5A pp. 11–13; Pupil's Book p. 11

Shared reading and writing

- Read the poems on pages 11–13 again with a view to using them as models or inspiration for the children's own poems. *League Division Fun* and *W* are "one-offs" which would be difficult to copy, but the remaining poems offer some good ideas.
- Discuss the suggestions in the Pupil's Book for using these poems as models.

Focused word/sentence work

- Look at the list of double words suggested by the children on day 1. Brainstorm further double words to add to the list. Sort them by rhyme, syllable count etc.

Independent work

- Children write their own poems.

Plenary

- Review the work in progress. Encourage the children to experiment with deleting words, adding words, changing words, reorganising words, and experimenting with figurative language.

DAY 4

Big Book 5A pp. 14–15; Pupil's Book pp. 10–11

Shared reading and writing

- Read the concrete poems on pages 14–15 in the Big Book and page 10 in the Pupil's Book. What do they have in common? How are they different?
- Would these poems be as successful if they were written as conventional poems? Ask the children to give reasons for their answers. Try rewriting the Shel Silverstein poem to test this. How would writing *Waves* in a conventional way have ruined the point of the final verse?
- Which is the most difficult poem to read? Why? Do the children think it might have been difficult to write? What makes them think so?
- Discuss the ideas for concrete poems on page 11 in the Pupil's Book.

Focused word/sentence work

- Explore *-ing* words which describe the same thing, e.g. as in *Waves*: *wallowing, billowing* waves. Ask the children to suggest *-ing* words for other things, e.g. *snow, rain, flying birds, smoke, an express train* etc. Discuss differences in shades of meaning.

Independent work

- Children continue writing poems, including concrete poems.

Plenary

- Review the children's work, offering help and encouragement.

DAY 5

Big Book 5A pp. 11–15; Pupil's Book pp. 10–11

Shared reading

- Compare the two Shel Silverstein poems *The Silver Fish* and the untitled poem written on the neck of a giraffe. How are they similar? How are they different?
- Which of the concrete poems do the children like best? Why? Ask them to refer to details and examples in the poem.
- Which of all the poems in this unit do they like best? Why?
- Which do they like least? Ask them to give reasons for their answers.

Focused word/sentence work

- Discuss the plurals of words ending in *f* and *y*. Ask the children to construct their own rules from paired singular and plural words, e.g. *loaf – loaves, berry – berries, baby – babies*. Note exceptions to the rule for changing *f* to *ve* before adding *s*, e.g. *roofs, chiefs, beliefs, dwarfs*.

Independent work

- Children continue writing poems.

Plenary

- Ask the children to read their poems to the class.
- Display their concrete poems for discussion.

Consolidation and extension

- Make a class anthology of the children's poems.
- Compare poems by the same author, identifying what is distinctive about the style and contents of their poems.
- Discuss the children's favourite poets. Ask them to say why they like them, referring to details and examples in the poems.
- Copymaster 7 is designed to help the children compare poems by the same author.

Homework

- Page 4 in the Homework Book investigates the plurals of words ending in *f* and *y*.

Unit 4 — The BFG

Key Learning Objectives

TL5 To understand dramatic conventions including:
- the conventions of scripting (e.g. stage directions, asides)
- how character can be communicated in words and gesture
- how tension can be built up through pace, silence and delivery

TL12 To discuss the enduring appeal of established authors

TL14 To map out texts showing development and structure, e.g. its high and low points, the links between sections, paragraphs, chapters

TL18 To write own playscript, applying conventions learned from reading; including production notes

TL19 To annotate a section of playscript as a preparation for performance, taking into account pace, movement, gesture and delivery of lines, and the needs of the audience

TL20 To evaluate the script and the performance for their dramatic interest and impact

SL7 From reading, to understand how dialogue is set out

WL7 To explain the differences between synonyms, and collect, classify and order sets of words to identify shades of meaning

WL10 To use adverbs to qualify verbs in writing dialogue, using a thesaurus to extend vocabulary

Range:	Playscripts; novels by significant children's writers
Texts:	From *Roald Dahl's The BFG – plays for children*, adapted by David Wood From *The BFG*, Roald Dahl
Resources:	Big Book 5A pp. 16–19 Pupil's Book 5 pp. 12–14 Homework Book 5 p. 5: Synonyms Copymasters 8 and 9: Glossary of language terms Copymaster 10: How a story develops

Preparation

- Make a thesaurus available for day 5, preferably *Collins Junior Thesaurus*.

DAY 1

Big Book 5A pp. 16–17; Pupil's Book pp. 12–13

Shared reading

- Discuss the conventions of scripting. How is the scene indicated, the action introduced and the dialogue set out? How are the stage directions presented? Identify directions for sound effects and lighting.
- How is the passing of time shown? How are the actions of the characters indicated? How important are pauses in the action?
- Discuss the use of italics in the dialogue. What does this indicate to the reader?

Focused word/sentence work

- Compare the different conventions for playscript and story book dialogue.
- Experiment with changing the dialogue into reported speech, e.g. *Mary wished the Queen good morning and offered her early-morning tea. The Queen said that she had had a most frightful dream.*

Independent work

- Children answer questions on the play.

Plenary

- Review the children's independent text work.

DAY 2

Big Book 5A pp. 16–17; Pupil's Book p. 13

Shared reading

- How is the audience made aware that Mary has realised something the Queen has not? How do Mary's words and reactions help to build up tension?
- Ask the children to read the playscript aloud, with one child reading the stage directions.
- Experiment with different interpretations of the dialogue, e.g. Mary as timid, confident, old etc.

Focused word/sentence work

- Ask the children to change the playscript dialogue into direct speech.
- Experiment with using adverbs to indicate how the words are spoken, e.g. *"Good morning, Your Majesty," said Mary brightly/timidly/softly/cheerfully.*

Independent work

- Children explore the use of adverbs to qualify verbs in writing dialogue.

Plenary

- Review the children's work on adverbs, re-emphasising teaching points and clarifying misconceptions.

DAY 3

Big Book 5A pp. 16–17; Pupil's Book p. 14

Shared reading and writing

- Read the text again. What might happen next? Which new characters might be introduced?
- Plan a continuation of the scene, applying playscript conventions.

Focused word/sentence work

- Point out the use of the apostrophe in "ma'am". Why is it there?
- Remind the children of the use of the apostrophe in contractions, e.g. *I've, you're, mustn't, isn't*.

Independent work

- Children begin work on continuing the playscript.

Plenary

- Review the work in progress, offering help and encouragement.

DAY 4

Big Book 5A pp. 18–19; Pupil's Book p. 14

Shared reading

- Compare the text of the original story by Roald Dahl with the earlier playscript adaptation. In what ways are they similar or different?
- Why wasn't Sophie mentioned in the playscript?
- From whose point of view is the story being told?
- Why is sound so important in this extract? Which words and phrases tell us what Sophie hears?
- What are we told about Mary which the playscript does not tell us?

Focused word/sentence work

- Investigate the past tense of the verb "to dream". Notice that "dreamed" is also acceptable.
- Ask the children to explain the difference between "were putting" and "put".
- Change the Queen's dream into a prophecy of what will happen in the future, e.g. *I dreamt that girls and boys will be snatched ...*

Independent work

- Children continue their playscripts.

Plenary

- Ask the children to read aloud or act out their playscripts.

DAY 5

Big Book 5A pp. 16–19; Pupil's Book p. 14

Shared reading

- Compare the story and the script from the point after the Queen says, "So *real.*" What different sounds do we hear? Why do you think the play introduces a different sound? Would the rattle of a tray work better than silence in the story version? Why does it work better in the playscript? How does the book version help to build the tension?
- Why is the dialogue in the playscript shorter than in the book? Why are some lines left out altogether?
- Discuss reasons why Roald Dahl's books are so popular.

Focused word/sentence work

- Use a thesaurus to find synonyms for words in the text, e.g. *pluck, awful, rattle, eat, vivid, real, quivering.*
- Discuss the differences in shades of meaning.

Independent work

- Children explore synonyms.

Plenary

- Review the week's work, re-emphasising teaching points and clarifying misconceptions.

Consolidation and extension

- Encourage the children to annotate their playscripts as preparation for performance, taking into account pace, movement, gesture and delivery of lines, and the needs of the audience.
- Encourage them to evaluate the script and their performance for their dramatic interest and impact.
- Collect, classify and order sets of words to identify shades of meaning.
- Copymasters 8 and 9, when copied back-to-back and folded, will make a useful four-page glossary of language terms.
- Copymaster 10 encourages the children to record the high and low points in stories.

Homework

- Page 5 in the Homework Book focuses on synonyms.

27

Unit 5   The Phantom Sausage Stealer

Key Learning Objectives

TL1	To analyse the features of a good opening
TL3	To investigate how characters are presented
TL5	To understand dramatic conventions including: – the conventions of scripting (e.g. stage directions, asides) – how character can be communicated in words and gesture – how tension can be built up through pace, silence and delivery
TL8	To investigate and collect different examples of wordplay, relating form to meaning
TL18	To write own playscript, applying conventions learned from reading, including production notes
TL19	To annotate a section of playscript as a preparation for performance, taking into account pace, movement, gesture and delivery of lines, and the needs of the audience
TL20	To evaluate the script and the performance for their dramatic interest and impact
SL8	To revise and extend work on verb forms: active, interrogative, imperative
WL6	To collect and investigate the meanings and spellings of words using the following prefixes: *auto, bi, trans, tele, circum*

Range:	Playscripts
Texts:	From *The Phantom Sausage Stealer*, Johnny Ball
Resources:	Big Book 5A pp. 20–25 Pupil's Book 5 pp. 15–17 Homework Book 5 p. 6: Statements, questions and orders

DAY 1

Big Book 5A pp. 20–23; Pupil's Book pp. 15–16

Shared reading

* This script is one of many sketches that Johnny Ball wrote for TV.
* Identify the conventions of scripting: list of characters, scene description, stage directions, asides, sound effects etc. What does the word "wings" mean?
* Which is the first clue that this play is a comedy? How does Golightly's struggling to see out of the window help to make the scene more amusing? Which words does she speak to herself? How does her running commentary build tension?
* In what way is Treadheavy's entrance dramatic? To what extent do Golightly's earlier running commentary and the off-stage sounds prepare us for it? Why is it still a surprise when he enters in the basket of a delivery boy's bicycle? Do the children think an audience would enjoy his entrance so much without the earlier preparation?
* Do the children think this is a good opening? Why?

Focused word/sentence work

* Discuss the meaning in context of the words *phantom, rotund, bubbly, efficient*.
* Discuss synonyms for these words.
* Ask the children to identify an example of non-standard English in the dialogue, e.g. *me back*.

Independent work

* Children answer questions on the text.

Plenary

* Review the children's independent text work.

DAY 2

Big Book 5A pp. 20–23; Pupil's Book p. 16

Shared reading

* What examples of wordplay are there? Why has the writer used the names Treadheavy and Golightly? Ask the children to explain the bent copper joke.
* Which seems to be the more important in this script, dialogue or action? Ask the children to suggest why this is so.
* Investigate how the characters are presented, e.g. through description in the cast list, dialogue and action.
* Make a list of props which the scene requires.

Focused word/sentence work

* Ask the children to identify words in the text with the prefixes *tele* and *bi* (e.g. *telephone* and *bike* (bicycle)). Ask the children to suggest other words with these prefixes. Make a list. Ask the children to work out what each prefix means.
* Introduce the children to the prefixes *auto, trans* and *circum*. Again make a list of words made from them and ask the children to work out the meaning.

Independent work

* Children investigate the meanings and spellings of words using the prefixes *auto, bi, trans, tele* and *circum*.

Plenary

* Review the children's work on prefixes. Discuss how the children arrived at their answers for section C. Challenge the class to find more words with these prefixes.

DAY 3

Big Book 5A pp. 20–23; Pupil's Book p. 17

Shared reading and writing, including focused word/sentence work

* Ask the children to read the text aloud.
* Discuss how the story might continue. Why might the delivery boy have come to the police station? What clues does the title give?
* Plan together a continuation of the playscript. Remind the children of dramatic conventions. Aim for consistency of character and style. Encourage the use of puns: the worse the better!

Independent work

* Children begin writing their playscripts.

Plenary

* Review the work in progress, offering help and encouragement.

DAY 4

Big Book 5A pp. 24–25; Pupil's Book p. 17

Shared reading

* Read the second extract from the playscript. What does the humour of this scene hinge on?
* What does Golightly do and say to show that she is a "bubbly policewoman trying hard to be efficient"? How can we tell that she has not realised her mistake in issuing a description of sausages instead of a thief? At what point does she begin to suspect that something is wrong? Which words tell us?
* Which words tell the reader how to say parts of the dialogue? What does "repeats without expression" mean?
* At what points does the writer indicate who is speaking to whom? Why is that important?

Focused word/sentence work

* Note the differences in the text between spoken and written English: hesitations ("er"), incomplete sentences ("Sausages in masks?").
* Note the use of dots in the punctuation. What is their function?
* What does the expression "walls have ears" mean?

Independent work

* Children continue work on their playscripts.

Plenary

* Discuss ways of annotating the children's playscripts as preparation for performance, taking into account pace, movement, gesture and delivery of lines, and the needs of the audience.

DAY 5

Big Book 5A pp. 24–25; Pupil's Book p. 17

Shared reading

* Ask the children to explain the pun "bangers and mashks".
* Why is "Intercom" listed as a character name?
* Do the children think this script is funny? Ask them to give reasons for their answers.
* Ask the children to read the scene aloud. Encourage them to use the stage directions to modify their delivery.

Focused word/sentence work

* Ask the children to identify statements, questions and orders in the text.
* Experiment with transforming one kind of sentence into another. What word changes are necessary?

Independent work

* Children consolidate the work on statements, questions and orders.

Plenary

* Review the week's work, consolidating teaching points, re-emphasising teaching points and clarifying misconceptions.

Consolidation and extension

* Ask the children to prepare a performance of their playscripts. Encourage them to annotate them, taking into account pace, movement, gesture and delivery of lines, and the needs of the audience.
* Encourage the children to evaluate the script and their performance for dramatic interest and impact.
* Ask the children to collect examples of wordplay from their reading, or from radio and TV. Discuss the relationship between form and meaning.

Homework

* Page 6 in the Homework Book focuses on statements, questions and orders, using the active, interrogative and imperative forms of verbs.

Unit 6 Diaries and Reports

Key Learning Objectives

TL4	To consider how texts can be rooted in the writer's experience
TL9	To develop an active attitude towards reading: seeking answers, anticipating events, empathising with characters and imagining events that are described
TL21	To identify the features of recounted texts (a diary and a sports report)
TL24	To write recounts based on personal experiences
TL26	To make notes as a record of what has been read
WL8	To identify word roots, derivations and spelling patterns

Range:	Recounts of events: diary, sports report
Texts:	From *The Diary of Anne Frank* Sports report: *United's cup hopes dashed*
Resources:	Big Book 5A pp. 26–30 Pupil's Book 5 pp. 18–20 Homework Book 5 p. 7: Joining sentences Copymaster 11: Anne Frank's Diary

Preparation

- Introduce the children to the background of the diary of Anne Frank. It tells a unique story and its survival is remarkable. When the family were arrested by the SS, and the annex searched, her diary was left untouched.

DAY 1

Big Book 5A pp. 26–28; Pupil's Book pp. 18–19

Shared reading

- Read the diary to the children. Then ask the children to take turns in reading an entry at a time. What picture of life in Amsterdam during the occupation do we get from Anne's writing? Why is her diary such an important document? Talk about what life must have been like for Anne and other Jews living in the city at the time.
- What impression do we get of Anne herself? Ask the children to pick out words and phrases which tell us about her thoughts and feelings.
- Which events in the diary are particularly frightening? Why?

Focused word/sentence work

- Revise verb tense. Ask the children to identify verbs from the text in the past, present and future tenses.
- Identify the auxiliary verbs, e.g. *is* huffing, *will be* interested, *has* received, *was* coming, *have* been.

Independent work

- Children answer questions on the text.

Plenary

- Review the children's independent text work. Make sure the children have understood fully why the Franks went into hiding.

DAY 2

Big Book 5A pp. 26–28; Pupil's Book pp. 18–19

Shared reading

- Discuss why the diary has such lasting appeal. Consider its historical value, its drama, how it reveals Anne as a real-life person, and how her description of her life touches the reader.
- Investigate the characteristics of diary writing: each entry dated, a first person account, a mix of past and present tense, and the expression of facts and opinions. Investigate how facts and opinions are represented in the text.

Focused word/sentence work

- Discuss the difference between autobiographical writing and biographical writing. Biographers often use diaries as research material. Experiment with transforming the first person diary into a third person account. Investigate the effects of changes on sentence structure, agreement with verbs, and meaning.

Independent work

- Children transform the first person diary into a third person account.

Plenary

- Review the children's third person accounts based on Anne's diary. Discuss the effects of changes on sentence structure, agreement with verbs and meaning.

DAY 3

Big Book 5A pp. 26–28; Pupil's Book p. 20

Shared reading and writing, including focused word/sentence work

- Discuss the features of the diary as a recounted text: an introduction to orientate the reader, chronological sequence, the use of words and phrases to indicate this chronology, e.g. *now*, *yesterday*, *at eight o'clock*.
- What is the purpose of Anne's diary? Who is her audience? What makes the children think so?
- Encourage the children to begin their own diary as an ongoing writing activity outside the literacy hour, or for homework. Discuss purpose and audience. Encourage them to express their opinions and feelings about events.
- Choose a recent event the children are all familiar with. Discuss different ways of recounting this. Consider purpose, audience and form, e.g. a newspaper report, an article for the school magazine, personal notes, a letter to a friend etc. Discuss how the degree of formality will differ, and how it will determine the choice of vocabulary, sentence structure etc. Experiment with different styles.

Independent work

- Children write a recount of a recent event, and will later begin their own diary.

Plenary

- Review the work in progress, offering help and encouragement.

DAY 4

Big Book 5A pp. 26–28; Pupil's Book p. 20

Shared reading and writing

- Read Anne's diary again. Note that it is written in complete sentences, but often diaries are written in note form. Why might that be? Why might Anne have written hers more fully? (She had lots of time on her hands, and the writing was educational.)
- Experiment with rewriting the first three entries from Anne's diary in note form.

Focused word/sentence work

- Identify the word "discovered" in the introduction. Which root word does it come from? How many other words can be made from it by adding prefixes and suffixes? What is the meaning of "cover"? How are words such as "discover" and "uncover" related to it?

Independent work

- Children complete their recounts from day 3 and then transform parts of Anne's diary into note form.

Plenary

- Review the children's recounts or notes. Emphasise the importance of chronological sequence in the reports, and awareness of audience. Notes should be clear and concise.

DAY 5

Big Book 5A pp. 29–30; Pupil's Book p. 20

Shared reading

- Read the newspaper sports report. Ask the children to identify how the reader is introduced to the match.
- Which words and phrases show the chronology in the report?
- Which words and phrases bring the report to life? Which of them are typical of a sports report?
- Investigate the style of the report. Who is it written for? How can the children tell? Is the report from a local or a national paper? Ask the children to explain their answers.
- Compare this recount to Anne Frank's diary. Consider purpose, audience, degree of formality, organisation and layout.

Focused word/sentence work

- Identify the word "impressive". What is its root word? Investigate words which are related to it, e.g. *express, expression, depress, pressure.*

Independent work

- Children explore word roots and spelling patterns in order to extend vocabulary and provide support for spelling.

Plenary

- Review the week's work, re-emphasising teaching points and clarifying misconceptions.

Consolidation and extension

- Collect examples of recounts from newspapers, magazines and books. Encourage the children to use them as models for their own writing, or for making notes.
- Ask the children to watch a school match, making notes for a short report for the class to enjoy.
- Experiment with changing the style of reports to adapt them for a younger audience.
- Copymaster 11 encourages the children to write further entries for Anne Frank's diary, beginning where the last extract left off. A number of ideas are suggested for the children to think about and discuss. Before they begin writing, ask the children to read her diary again to re-familiarise themselves with her style.
- Ask the children to read aloud their new entries for Anne's diary. Discuss how successful they are in style and content.

Homework

- Page 7 in the Homework Book gives practice in using a wide range of conjunctions when joining sentences.

Unit 7 Instructions

Key Learning Objectives

TL22	To read and evaluate a range of instructional texts in terms of their purpose, organisation and layout
TL23	To discuss the purpose of note-taking and how this influences the nature of notes made
TL25	To write instructional texts, and test them out
TL26	To make notes for different purposes, e.g. noting key points as a record of what has been read, listing cues for a talk, and to build on these notes in their own writing or speaking
TL27	To use simple abbreviations in note-taking
SL3	To discuss, proofread and edit their own writing for clarity and correctness
SL9	To identify the imperative form in instructional writing and the past tense in recounts and use this awareness when writing for these purposes

Range:	Instructional texts: rules, instructions
Texts:	From *Liquid Magic*, Philip Watson Growing Seeds
Resources:	Big Book 5A pp. 31–34 Pupil's Book 5 pp. 21–23 Homework Book 5 p. 8: Writing a report

Preparation

- Although it is not essential to carry out the instructions in the Big Book, the learning experience will be enriched if you do so.

- For safety reasons children should follow carefully the laboratory procedure rules listed on page 32 in the Big Book.

- For the dancing mothballs experiment (day 1 or 2) you will need: 5–6 mothballs, spirit-based felt-tipped pens, a large glass jar and water, 10 tablespoons of vinegar, 2 teaspoons of sodium bicarbonate and a wooden spoon.

- For growing seeds (day 4 or 5) you will need: apple, orange, lemon pips or similar; conkers, acorns, sycamore seeds or similar; yogurt pots or similar; potting compost; a pencil; small plastic bags.

DAY 1

Big Book 5A pp. 31–32; Pupil's Book pp. 21–22

Shared reading

- Read the laboratory procedure rules. What is their purpose? How are they organised? Why are they numbered? Are they clear and useful? Ask the children to explain why each rule is necessary.

- What is the purpose of the mothballs experiment? How are the instructions organised? What is the purpose of the first and last paragraphs? Are the instructions clear and useful?

- Compare the experiment text with the procedure rules. How are they similar and different?

- Ask the children to suggest ideas for a short introduction to the laboratory procedure rules.

Focused word/sentence work

- Investigate the use of the present tense, the imperative form (for giving instructions, advice), and the second person in procedural texts. Compare this with a recounted text (report).

Independent work

- Children answer questions on the text.

Plenary

- Review the children's independent text work.

DAY 2

Big Book 5A pp. 31–32; Pupil's Book pp. 21–22

Shared reading

- Conduct the mothballs experiment. Which of the laboratory rules need to be observed here? Why?

- After the experiment, discuss how clear the instructions proved to be.

- Show the children how to make notes of the instructions.

Focused word/sentence work

- What are the differences between the recount and the instructions? (e.g. verb tense, person and form).

- Explain how the materials may be listed in a sentence, using a colon to signal the list, e.g. *You will need: 5 or 6 mothballs, ...*

Independent work

- Children make notes on the mothball instructions and the laboratory rules. These notes will be needed on day 5.

Plenary

- Ask the children to recount orally what they did in the experiment.

- Review the children's independent work. Emphasise the need to include all the important points. Suggest ways of making the notes more concise.

DAY 3

Big Book 5A pp. 31–32; Pupil's Book p. 23

Shared reading and writing

- Use the instructions in the anthology as a model to plan, draft, edit and refine instructions linked to work in other subjects.

- Choose a subject from the ones listed in the Pupil's Book, or one popular with the children. Discuss how to organise the instructions, e.g. headings, an introduction, list of materials, sequencing, and whether diagrams might help make things clearer. Is there any need to include a safety warning?

- Begin writing the instructions. Encourage the children to check at each stage that the instructions are sufficiently clear.

- Check to see that everything is in the right order, and that nothing has been left out.

Focused word/sentence work

- Make the children aware of the use of the imperative form in instructional writing (second person and present tense).

Independent work

- Children begin writing their own instructions.

Plenary

- Review the work in progress, offering help and encouragement.
- Ask the children to exchange their writing with a classmate for evaluation.

DAY 4

Big Book 5A pp. 33–34; Pupil's Book p. 23

Shared reading

- Read the instructions for growing seeds. Note the organisation and layout of the text: identification of outcome at the start, a list of materials needed, a method with clear stages and sequential layout with numbered points, the use of diagrams and headings.
- In what ways is the organisation and layout of this text similar to the earlier texts in this unit, or to other procedural texts, e.g. recipes, rules for games?

Focused word/sentence work

- Experiment with transforming this text into a report. What changes are needed? (e.g. use of the past tense, active form, and the first or third person).

Independent work

- Children complete their instructions. They will need time outside the literacy hour to test their instructions, perhaps as homework.

Plenary

- Review the children's instructions with regard to purpose, layout and organisation, clarity and usefulness.

DAY 5

Big Book 5A pp. 31–34; Pupil's Book p. 23

Shared reading

- Carry out the instructions for growing seeds with the children. Which laboratory rules should be observed? Why?
- Are the instructions clear? Have the children any suggestions for improving them?
- Ask the children to recount orally what they did in the experiment.

Focused word/sentence work

- Investigate the spelling pattern *struct* in the word "instruction". Ask the children to add prefixes and suffixes to this pattern to make new words, e.g. *construct, structure, destruction*.

Independent work

- Children use their notes from day 2 to reconstruct instructions for the mothballs experiment and the laboratory rules.
- The extension suggestion, making notes for a two-minute talk to the class, may be done outside the literacy hour, or as homework.

Plenary

- Review the week's work, consolidating teaching points.

Consolidation and extension

- Discuss how the purpose of note-taking influences the nature of the notes, e.g. noting the materials needed as preparation for the mothballs experiment; making notes of the results of the experiment for a written report.
- Allow time for the children to test their own written instructions.
- Display the children's instructions for discussion and evaluation.
- Collect other examples of instructional texts for discussion, comparison, and as models for further writing.
- Compare the children's reports (see homework below) with the original procedural text in the anthology. How are they different?

Homework

- Page 8 in the Homework Book reproduces the instructions for growing seeds. The pupil is asked to rewrite these instructions as a report on the completed activity. This gives practice in changing verbs from imperative to active, from second to first person, and from present to past tense. Encourage the children to use a wide range of connectives in their writing.

Bears and Lions

Key Learning Objectives

TL3	To investigate how characters are presented
TL4	To consider how texts can be rooted in the writer's experience
TL9	To develop an active attitude towards reading: seeking answers, anticipating events, empathising with characters and imagining events that are described
TL23	To discuss the purpose of note-taking and how this influences the nature of notes made
TL26	To make notes for different purposes
TL27	To use simple abbreviations in note-taking
SL2	To understand the basic conventions of standard English and consider when and why standard English is used
SL4	To adapt writing for different readers and purposes by changing vocabulary, tone and sentence structure to suit, simplifying for younger readers
SL6	To understand the need for punctuation as an aid to the reader
SL8	To revise and extend work on verb tenses, past, present, future; investigating how different tenses are formed by using auxiliary verbs

Range:	Novels by significant children's writers
Texts:	From *The Dancing Bear*, and *Tom's Sausage Lion*, Michael Morpurgo
Resources:	Big Book 5A pp. 35–38 Pupil's Book 5 pp. 24–26 Homework Book 5 p. 9: Proofreading Copymaster 12: Story board

Preparation

- The two extracts in this unit are from books by Michael Morpurgo. The idea for *The Dancing Bear* (Collins) came from a holiday in the Pyrenees. There he came across a bear in a cage in a small village. The bear had been found as an orphan cub and brought up by a girl.

DAY 1

Big Book 5A pp. 35–36; Pupil's Book pp. 24–25

Shared reading

- Discuss how the idea for this story is rooted in the writer's experience (see preparation above).

- How is Roxanne presented to the reader: through action, dialogue, description, or a combination? How do the children respond to her? How would they feel in her position?

- Investigate how her grandfather is presented. How do the children feel towards him? How might he have behaved differently if others had not been there when Roxanne arrrived with the bear? Would such action be justified? Ask the children to explain their answers.

Focused word/sentence work

- Investigate the use of punctuation in the text, e.g. commas, dashes, colons, apostrophes denoting possession and contraction, double and single inverted commas.

- Experiment with changing the direct speech into reported speech. Note the changes which have to be made, e.g. "He's my very own bear, Grandpa" becomes *Roxanne told her grandfather that the bear was her very own.* What would be confusing in the sentence "Roxanne told her grandfather that *he* was her very own"?

Independent work

- Children answer questions on the text.

Plenary

- Review the children's independent text work. Discuss the children's opinion of Roxanne's grandfather.

DAY 2

Big Book 5A pp. 35–36; Pupil's Book p. 25

Shared reading

- Why do the children think the narrator persuaded her grandfather to keep the bear? What do the words "I was still thinking hard" tell us?

- Ask the children to imagine they are newspaper reporters sent to make notes for a news report. Discuss which information from the text they will need. Point out that the purpose of note-taking influences the nature of the notes made.

- Discuss how to use abbreviations in notes, e.g. using R for Roxanne once her name has been noted in full.

Focused word/sentence work

- Investigate word order. Change the word order in each of the four sentences in paragraph one. What changes are necessary to keep the same meaning? Investigate shortening the sentences. Identify the words which are essential to meaning. Which words may be deleted without damaging the basic meaning?

Independent work

- Children make notes on the story in preparation for writing a newspaper report about it.

Plenary

- Review the children's notes and newspaper report. Discuss how the purpose of the note-taking influenced the nature of the notes.

DAY 3

Big Book 5A pp. 35–36; Pupil's Book p. 26

Shared reading and writing, including focused word/sentence work

- Ask the children to read the story aloud, using punctuation as an aid to their reading.

- Tell the children that they are going to write a new version of the story for younger readers. Ask them to think of someone they know well to write the story for, a younger member of the family or someone at school. With this particular audience in mind, ask them which aspects of the story would be most interesting to their reader. Which would be least interesting? Ask them to give reasons for their answers.

- To help with simplifying the story, read some of the notes and/or news reports the children wrote on day 2. These will already have picked out the most important incidents.

- Make a story plan with a young audience in mind, concentrating on those parts they would be most likely to find interesting.

- Tell the story from Roxanne's point of view, as younger children will find it easy to identify with her. Encourage the children to describe how she felt at different points in the story. Decide which is more appropriate for this version: a first or a third person account. Discuss ways of ending the story.

- Talk about the need to use language the children will understand and enjoy.

Independent work
- Children begin their story for a younger audience.
- Copymaster 12 is a story board which the children will find useful to help with planning their story.

Plenary
- Review the work in progress, with particular emphasis on structure and vocabulary. Have the children included any detail which younger children might find difficult or uninteresting?

- If any of the children have written for younger pupils in the school, make arrangements with their teachers for your children to read their completed stories to the younger ones at a convenient time.

DAY 4

Big Book 5A pp. 37–38; Pupil's Book p. 26

Shared reading
- Read the extract from Michael Morpurgo's *Tom's Sausage Lion*. How is this extract similar to the earlier one? How is it different?

- To what extent might the writer be drawing on his experience as a teacher?

- How is Barry presented to the reader? How does Tom appear to have got on with him previously? What makes the children think so? How have the tables now been turned? Does Tom appear to be enjoying the situation? How can the children tell?

- How do the children feel about the way Barry is being treated?

Focused word/sentence work
- Ask the children to read the story aloud, using punctuation as an aid to their reading.

- Investigate word order. Identify the words which are essential to meaning, and which words may be deleted without damaging the basic meaning.

Independent work
- Children continue their stories.

Plenary
- Ask the children to read their stories aloud to the class for evaluation. If convenient, ask them to visit children in a younger class and read to them.

DAY 5

Big Book 5A pp. 37–38; Pupil's Book p. 26

Shared reading
- Do the children think this might be a true story? What makes them think so?

- Are the other children in the playground behaving as they would if a real lion had arrived there? How would the children in your class feel and behave if it happened to them?

- Discuss what might happen next in the story.

Focused word/sentence work
- Investigate verb tense. Ask the children to pick examples of past, present and future tense verbs.

- Discuss the use of auxiliary verbs in forming tenses: *was, were, has, have, had, did, is, are, am, will* and *shall*. Ask the children to identify auxiliary verbs in the text. Which tense does each help to form?

Independent work
- Children practise using auxiliary verbs to form the past and present tenses.

Plenary
- Review the week's work, re-emphasising teaching points and clarifying misconceptions.

Consolidation and extension

- Make time available for the children to illustrate their stories.

- Arrange with teachers of younger children for members of your class to visit them at convenient times to read and talk about their stories.

- Copymaster 12 is a story board to help the children with story planning.

Homework

- Page 9 in the Homework Book gives practice in proofreading and correcting work for grammatical errors.

Unit 9   Classic Stories

Key Learning Objectives

TL1	To analyse the features of a good opening and compare a number of story openings
TL3	To investigate how characters are presented
TL11	To experiment with alternative ways of opening a story using e.g. description, action or dialogue
TL12	To discuss the enduring appeal of established authors and "classic" texts
SL1	To investigate word order
SL6	To understand the need for punctuation as an aid to the reader, e.g. commas to mark grammatical boundaries; a colon to signal e.g. a list

Range:	Novels by significant children's writers: classic texts
Range:	From *The Railway Children*, E. Nesbit From *The Secret Garden*, Frances Hodgson Burnett
Resources:	Big Book 5A pp. 39–43 Pupil's Book 5 pp. 27–29 Homework Book 5 p. 10: Word order Copymaster 13: Books with lasting appeal

DAY 1

Big Book 5A pp. 39–41; Pupil's Book pp. 27–28

Shared reading

- How are the characters introduced: through dialogue, action or description? Note that we learn about the railway children more from the description of their parents and their house than from direct description of the children themselves. To show this, ask the class what they know about Peter. How much of this are we told directly? How much are we told indirectly?
- How do the children get on with their parents? What evidence is there for this in the text?
- How does the class respond to the children? Do they think the railway children are lucky? Why?

Focused word/sentence work

- Investigate sentence length in the extract. Most sentences are long, as is often the case in older literature. Other sentences are short, in particular the first and last sentences. Discuss the effect of the short sentence: "The dreadful change came quite suddenly."
- Ask the children to identify the use of dashes in the text, and of a colon to signal a list.

Independent work

- Children answer questions on the text.

Plenary

- Review the children's independent text work, with particular emphasis on section C. How successful is the story opening in making the reader want to read on? Ask the children to explain their answers.

DAY 2

Big Book 5A pp. 39–41; Pupil's Book p. 28

Shared reading

- What is the main idea of each paragraph? How are the paragraphs linked?
- At what point do we realise that the children's life is going to change completely? Which words tell us? What does the class think the change might be? What might cause that change?
- Ask those who have read the book, or have seen the film, why this book has lasting appeal. Is it the characters, the setting or the action? Or is it a mixture of some or all of these things?

Focused word/sentence work

- Explain to the children that a clause is a part of a sentence with its own verb. A complex sentence is made up of two clauses, a main clause and a second or subordinate clause. A simple sentence can be made into a complex sentence by adding a clause, e.g. "He bought a cottage *where he could spend his weekends*."
- Give the children a variety of simple sentences to make into complex sentences by adding a clause.

Independent work

- Children practise creating complex sentences by adding clauses.

Plenary

- Review the children's work on complex sentences. If the children have used phrases instead of clauses, explain that a clause contains a verb. In the sentence "I can't go out *until five o'clock*" the italicised words make a phrase, whereas in "I can't go out *until I have finished my work*" the italicised words are a clause.

DAY 3

Big Book 5A pp. 39–41; Pupil's Book p. 29

Shared reading and writing, including focused word/sentence work

- How does this story open: with dialogue, action or description? Do the children think it is a good opening? Why? How is it similar to, or different from, the story openings in units 1 and 2? Does this opening make the children want to read on? Why?
- Read together the three alternative openings to the story on page 29 in the Pupil's Book. Which do they think works best? Why? Ask the children to identify words they find particularly effective.
- Experiment with three new openings to the story, using dialogue, action and description. Which of these do the children think works best? Why?

Independent work

- Children write alternative openings to a story.

Plenary

- Review the work in progress. Discuss the children's alternative openings to the story. Which work best? Why? Do any particular words or phrases contribute to this effect?

DAY 4

Big Book 5A pp. 42–43; Pupil's Book p. 29

Shared reading

- Read the extract from *The Secret Garden*. How is Mary presented: through dialogue, action or description? What kind of relationship does she have with her mother? Why? How do the children respond to Mary and her mother?

- How is this opening similar to, or different from, that of *The Railway Children*? Do the children think this is a good opening? Why? Does it make them want to read on? Ask them to explain their answers.

Focused word/sentence work

- What do the children think an *Ayah* and a *Memsahib* are? What makes them think so?

- Investigate suitable synonyms as substitutes for words in the text, e.g. *light* hair, *sour* expression, *ill*, *ugly*.

Independent work

- Children choose one of their opening paragraphs and write three more to complete the story.

Plenary

- Review the children's stories in an atmosphere of constructive criticism.

DAY 5

Big Book 5A pp. 39–43; Pupil's Book p. 29

Shared reading

- Which of the two openings do the children prefer, that of *The Secret Garden* or that of *The Railway Children*? Why?

- Ask the children to read aloud the opening they prefer, using knowledge of punctuation as an aid to their reading.

Focused word/sentence work

- Ask the children to identify and explain the use of commas in the text.

- Investigate word order. Experiment with changing the word order of selected sentences to retain meaning.

- Investigate how words can be deleted without damaging the basic meaning, e.g. the subordinate clause in the first sentence of the text. The basic meaning remains if this is deleted, but what information is lost?

Independent work

- Children explore changing the word order in sentences, to retain meaning, to change meaning, and to delete words to keep the same basic meaning.

Plenary

- Review the week's work, consolidating and re-emphasising teaching points and clarifying misconceptions.

Consolidation and extension

- Ask the children to plan and carry out a survey of the most popular books with children in your school. Ask them to do the same with the books adults enjoyed as children. Compare the two lists. Are there any titles in common? Ask the children to suggest reasons for this. How many books on the first list have the children seen in adaptations on film or TV? To what extent might such adaptations have influenced their inclusion in the list of favourites?

- Copymaster 13 invites the children to explore why books popular with earlier generations of children, such as *The Railway Children* and *The Secret Garden*, are still popular today. Ask the children to select a book with lasting appeal and to say why they enjoyed it. Then ask them to ask a known adult, who read the same book as a child, why he or she enjoyed it. This information should then help them to decide what it is that gives the book lasting appeal.

- Ask the children to investigate deleting the less important words in sentences from their reading, while retaining the basic meaning.

Homework

- Page 10 in the Homework Book gives practice in changing the word order of sentences to retain or change meaning.

Unit 10 All Sorts of Poems

Key Learning Objectives

TL7	To analyse and compare poetic style, use of forms and the themes of significant poets; to respond to shades of meaning; to explain and justify personal tastes; to consider the impact of full rhymes, half rhymes, internal rhymes and other sound patterns
TL16	To convey feelings, reflections or moods in a poem through the careful choice of words and phrases
TL17	To write metaphors from original ideas or from similes
SL6	To understand the need for punctuation as an aid to the reader
WL7	To explain the differences between synonyms, to collect, classify and order sets of words to identify shades of meaning

Range:	Poems by significant children's writers
Texts:	*Ant*, Zoë Bailey; *What is fog?*, John Foster; *What is … the Sun?*, Wes Magee; from *Paper Boats*, Rabindranath Tagore; *At the butterflies*, Issa; *Steel Band Jump Up*, Faustin Charles; *At Kisagata*, Matsuo Basho
Resources:	Big Book 5A pp. 44–48 Pupil's Book 5 pp. 30–33 Homework Book 5 p. 11: Proofreading for spelling and punctuation Copymaster 14: Revision – term 1 assessment master

Preparation

- In this unit the children will write poems on days 3, 4 and 5.

DAY 1

Big Book 5A pp. 44–46; Pupil's Book pp. 30–31

Shared reading

- Read and enjoy all three poems, then explore each in turn.
- How does the poem *Ant* make the children feel? Is the ant presented as a victim or a hero? What do the words "hiss and explode" remind the children of? What is the "Ark" in the poem? Why has the poet chosen this word?
- What three different "word pictures" does the poet paint in *What is fog?* Which do the children like best? Why?
- What are the five word pictures in *What is … the Sun?* Ask the children to explain them.
- Which poem do the children like best? Why?

Focused word/sentence work

- Collect sound words from *Ant*, e.g. *rattles, booms, hiss, explode*. Make a list of other sound words the children know. Classify them, e.g. into loud and soft sounds, words that are onomatopoeic. Identify and discuss shades of meaning.

Independent work

- Children answer questions about the poems.

Plenary

- Review the children's independent text work. Discuss their preferences.

DAY 2

Big Book 5A pp. 44–46; Pupil's Book pp. 30–31

Shared reading

- How are the ant's legs described? Explain that this description is a *simile*. A simile is when one thing is said to be like another. Similes contain the words "as" or "like". In the same poem identify the *metaphor* for a raindrop: "bright balloon of water". Explain that whereas a simile says a thing is *like* something else, a metaphor says a thing *is* something else.
- Which poems are similar? In what way are they similar? Explain to the children that *What is fog?* and *What is … the Sun?* are metaphor poems. Each verse features a different metaphor for its subject. Discuss the effectiveness of each one.

Focused word/sentence work

- Make a list of well-known similes, e.g. *as cold as ice*.
- Investigate how these can be changed into metaphors. Ask the children what things might be said to be *as cold as ice*, e.g. cold feet. A metaphor would say that such feet *were* ice, e.g. "my feet were blocks of ice". Is the metaphor more effective than the simile? Why?
- Encourage the children to suggest further metaphors for fog or the sun, e.g. the sun as a balloon. Experiment with metaphors for the moon or ice.

Independent work

- Children investigate similes and metaphors, and write their own metaphors from similes.

Plenary

- Review the children's work on similes and metaphors. Discuss the metaphors they made from similes. Recap on the difference between a simile and a metaphor.

DAY 3

Big Book 5A pp. 44–46; Pupil's Book pp. 30, 32, 33

Shared reading and writing, including focused word/sentence work

- Look at the ideas for poetry writing on page 33 in the Pupil's Book. Each one draws inspiration from one of the poems in this unit. Some poems may be used as models for the children's own poems. Choose either a metaphor poem or a poem about a busy creature for writing as a shared poem.
- Brainstorm ideas and make notes. Pick out the best ideas for your poem. Make notes of words and phrases you might use, especially metaphors. Re-read the poem,

which may be used as a model for your shared poem. Discuss ways of adapting its structure to your ideas. Begin writing your poem.

Independent work

- Children either complete the shared poem or write a poem of their own.

Plenary

- Review the work in progress, offering help and encouragement. Encourage the children to think of ways in which their poems might be improved.

DAY 4

Big Book 5A pp. 47–48; Pupil's Book pp. 32–33

Shared reading and writing

- Read the poems on pages 47–48 in the Big Book. Which is a haiku? How is *At Kisagata* similar to the haiku? How is it different?
- Which poem do the children like best? Why?
- Choose another idea from those on page 32 in the Pupil's Book for poetry writing.
- Brainstorm ideas and make notes. Pick out the best ideas for your poem. Re-read the original poem. Discuss ways of adapting its structure to your ideas. Begin writing your poem.

Focused word/sentence work

- Ask the children to identify the sound words in *Steel Band Jump Up*.

Independent work

- Children improve their poem from day 3, or begin work on a second poem.

Plenary

- Review the work in progress, offering help and encouragement.

DAY 5

Big Book 5A pp. 47–48; Pupil's Book pp. 30, 32, 33

Shared reading

- Which poem rhymes? What is its rhyming pattern? Is this a regular pattern? Tap or clap out its rhythm. Do any of the other poems have such a strong rhythm?
- What pictures do the poems make in your mind? How do they make you feel?
- Discuss with the children what makes a poem. Does a poem need to rhyme? Does it need a strong rhythm? Is it set out differently from stories or other texts? Does a poem need to be of a specific length? Does it need to follow a set pattern? Do some poems follow such patterns? What kinds of poem do so?
- Do poems make clear pictures in your mind? Do poets often choose words for their sound as well as their meaning? Do poems make you feel things strongly?
- What do the children like about poems? Ask them to give reasons for their answers.

Focused word/sentence work

- Ask the children to identify the internal half-rhyme in *Steel Band Jump Up* (*deep*, *sweet*).
- Investigate punctuation in the poems. Which poems use colons? In the poem *At Kisagata* the colon is used, not to signal a list, but to separate two statements where the second statement explains the result of the first.
- In which poem is each verse punctuated as a single sentence?
- Which poems use exclamation marks? Why?
- Which poem uses a semi-colon? A semi-colon is used to link two closely connected ideas.

Independent work

- Children write a third poem.
- Ask the children to prepare one of their poems for reading aloud.

Plenary

- Ask the children to read some of their poems aloud.
- Review the work done so far on similes and metaphors, re-emphasising teaching points and clarifying misconceptions.

Consolidation and extension

- Ask the children to collect examples of similes and metaphors from their reading.
- Reserve some time outside the literacy hour to discuss the children's collections of similes and metaphors. Which do the children like best? Why?
- Make an anthology of the children's poems.
- Ask the children to write a review of their classmates' poems, saying why they like them. Display the reviews with the poems.

Homework

- Page 11 in the Homework Book gives practice in proofreading for spelling and punctuation mistakes.

ASSESSMENT

Copymaster 14 is an assessment master of key word and sentence objectives for term 1, testing the children's ability to: use speech marks and other punctuation; change direct into reported speech; use auxiliary verbs in the past and future tenses; construct sentences of their own from given words and phrases. Indirectly, it will also test vocabulary, spelling and handwriting. The completed sheet will be useful as a record of progress, together with examples of the pupil's text work.

TERM 2

HALF TERMLY PLANNER

Year 5 • Term 2 • Weeks 1–5

SCHOOL _____ CLASS _____ TEACHER _____

		Phonetics, spelling and vocabulary	Grammar and punctuation	Comprehension and composition	Texts
Continuous work **Weeks 1–5**		WL 1, 2, 3	SL 2		**Range** **Fiction and poetry:** traditional stories, legends, fables from a range of cultures
Blocked work					
Week	**Unit**				**Titles**
1	11	WL 4, 11		TL 1, 11	From *Aesop's Fables* From *Fables of Africa*, retold by Jan Knappert
2	12	WL 6	SL 3, 6, 8	TL 1, 2, 3, 10, 11, 13, 24	From *King Arthur and His Knights of the Round Table*, retold by Roger Lancelyn Green From *King Arthur*, retold by Andrew Matthews and Peter Utton
3	13		SL 4, 6, 7, 10	TL 1, 3, 8, 14	From *The Adventures of Rama and Sita*, retold by Ruskin Bond
4	14		SL 4	TL 1, 20, 21, 22, 24	*Beasts from Myths and Legends* From *Giants and Warriors*, retold by James Reeves
5	15	WL 7	SL 4, 9	TL 1, 11, 13	From *Giants and Warriors*, retold by James Reeves

Focus on Literacy Teacher's Resource Book 5 © Barry and Anita Scholes, HarperCollins*Publishers* Ltd 1999

HALF TERMLY PLANNER

Year 5 • Term 2 • Weeks 6–10

SCHOOL _____ CLASS _____ TEACHER _____

	Phonetics, spelling and vocabulary	Grammar and punctuation	Comprehension and composition	Texts
Continuous work **Weeks 6–10**	WL 1, 2, 3	SL 2		**Range** **Fiction and poetry**: traditional stories, myths from a range of cultures; longer classic poetry, including narrative poetry **Non-fiction**: non-chronological reports; explanations of processes
Blocked work **Week** / **Unit**				**Titles**
6 / 16	WL 10, 12	SL 1, 8	TL 1, 9, 10, 11, 13, 24	From *West Indian Folk Tales*, retold by P. Sherlock; From *How Stories Came into the World*, retold by Joanna Troughton
7 / 17	WL 4, 9	SL 1, 5, 8, 9	TL 15, 16, 17, 18, 19, 20, 22, 23, 24	*Rain, Thunder and Lightning*
8 / 18	WL 5, 10		TL 4, 5, 6, 7, 10, 12	*Bishop Hatto*, Robert Southey
9 / 19	WL 8	SL 2, 7	TL 4, 5, 10, 12	*Matilda*, Hilaire Belloc From *The Boy Who Cried Wolf*, Tony Ross
10 / 20	WL 12	SL 5, 9	TL 2, 3, 8, 11, 13, 24	From *The Tale of Ali Baba and the Forty Thieves*, translated by Anthea Bell From *Turkish Folk-Tales*, retold by Barbara K. Walker

Unit 11 Fables

Key Learning Objectives

TL1   To identify and classify the features of fables

TL11   To write own versions of a myth using structures and themes identified in reading

WL4   To explore spelling patterns of consonants and formulate rules:
- *ll* in *full* becomes *l* when used as a suffix
- words ending with a single consonant preceded by a short vowel double the consonant before adding *-ing*
- *c* is usually soft when followed by *i*

WL11 To explore onomatopoeia; collect, invent and use words whose meaning is represented in their sounds

Range:	Fables
Texts:	From *Aesop's Fables* From *Fables of Africa* retold by Jan Knappert
Resources:	Big Book 5B pp. 4–7 Pupil's Book 5 pp. 34–36 Homework Book 5 p. 12: Words which sound like their meaning

DAY 1

Big Book 5B pp. 4–5; Pupil's Book pp. 34–35

Shared reading

- Why do the children think Aesop wrote his fables? What is the moral of each of these fables?
- Investigate how each fable teaches its moral.
- Ask the children to retell *The Dove and the Ant*. How is the oral version different from the written version? Discuss reasons for this.
- Which fable do the children like best? Why?

Focused word/sentence work

- Ask the children to suggest antonyms for words in the text, e.g. *stopped, aloud, careful, began, quickly, over, onto, afterward, opened, strong, arrived, delighted, shallow, long, in, went, thick, tall.*
- Encourage them to use some of the antonyms in sentences of their own.

Independent work

- Children answer questions about the fables.

Plenary

- Review the children's independent text work. Remind the children how to use the text to find literal answers, and how to use clues where information is not given directly.

DAY 2

Big Book 5B pp. 4–5; Pupil's Book p. 35

Shared reading

- Ask the children to retell *The Fox and the Stork*. How is the oral version different from the written version? Discuss reasons for this.
- Investigate ways of changing *The Dove and the Ant* so that it features a lion and a mouse.
- Change *The Fox and the Stork* so that it tells of a giraffe and a fox.

Focused word/sentence work

- Ask the children to identify the word "ouch" in the text. Explain that the meaning of this word is represented by its sound. The word is therefore an example of onomatopoeia. Brainstorm other words which are onomatopoeic, e.g. *crash, bang, hiss, chug, clash, pop, thud, tinkle, cuckoo, hoot, toot, jingle, clink.*
- Ask the children to put the words in sentences.

Independent work

- Children explore onomatopoeia.

Plenary

- Review the children's independent work, re-emphasising teaching points and clarifying misconceptions.

DAY 3

Big Book 5B pp. 4–5; Pupil's Book p. 36

Shared reading and writing, including focused word/sentence work

- Ask the children to identify and classify the features of a fable, e.g. its moral, how it opens and ends, its characters.
- Explain what a proverb is. Discuss suitable proverbs to use as the moral of a fable.
- Choose one of the proverbs listed on page 36 in the Pupil's Book to use in a shared writing fable. Which animal characters would best illustrate this moral? Which character would come out as the hero, and which the villain? What will happen in the story? How will the story begin?

Independent work

- Children begin writing their own fable.

Plenary

- Review the children's work on fables, offering help and encouragement.

DAY 4

Big Book 5B pp. 6–7; Pupil's Book p. 36

Shared reading

- Why did the wild pigeons pretend to be dead? How did this give the caged pigeon an idea?
- How is *The Man and His Pigeon* similar to the fables by Aesop? How is it different?
- What do the children think the moral of this fable is?

Focused word/sentence work

- Ask the children to identify the word "decided" in the text. What sound does the *c* have in this word? Point out that *c* is usually soft when followed by *i*. Ask the children to suggest other similar words, e.g. *circus, accident, circle, city.*

Independent work

- Children continue work on their fables.

Plenary

- Ask some children to read their fables aloud. Encourage them to evaluate their own and others' work, in an atmosphere of constructive criticism. Have the children begun and ended their stories in the traditional manner? Does the story illustrate the moral?

DAY 5

Big Book 5B pp. 6–7; Pupil's Book p. 36

Shared reading

- Ask the children to retell this fable in their own words. Compare the oral with the written version.
- Which of the three fables in this unit do the children prefer? Encourage them to give reasons for their answers.

Focused word/sentence work

- Give the children examples of words made by adding *full* as a suffix, e.g. *wonderful, hopeful, painful*. Make a list. Ask them to suggest further examples. Look at the spelling of those words. Ask the children to formulate a spelling rule for adding *full* to a root word.
- Do the same with single-syllable words ending in a single consonant, e.g. *trap, bat, clip, stop*. Ask the children to add the suffixes *-ing, -ed* or *-er* to the words on your list. Write down the new words they have made. Ask the children to formulate a spelling rule.

Independent work

- Children investigate the spelling changes when adding *full, -ing, -ed* or *-er* to a root word, and formulate rules.

Plenary

- Discuss the children's formulated rules. Are they accurate? Test them with words suggested by the children. Encourage the children to learn the rules.

Consolidation and extension

- Collect and read other fables. Ask the children to identify and classify their features.
- Compile the children's fables in a class anthology, with illustrations.
- Make a display of the children's collected examples of onomatopoeia, with suitable illustrations, and examples of their use.
- Encourage the children to invent their own onomatopoeic words.
- Display the children's formulated spelling rules, with examples.

Homework

- Page 12 in the Homework Book encourages further exploration of onomatopoeia.

Unit 12 King Arthur

Key Learning Objectives

TL1   To identify and classify the features of legends

TL2   To investigate different versions of the same story, indentifying similarities and differences; recognise how stories change over time

TL3   To explore similarities and differences between oral and written storytelling

TL10   To understand the differences between literal and figurative language

TL11   To write own versions of legends, using structures and themes identified in reading

TL13   To review and edit writing to produce a final form, matched to the needs of an identified reader

TL24   To evaluate their work

SL3   To understand how writing can be adapted for different audiences and purposes

SL6   To be aware of the differences between spoken and written language

SL8   To construct sentences in different ways, while retaining meaning

WL6   To distinguish between homophones

Range:	Different versions of the same legend
Texts:	From *King Arthur and His Knights of the Round Table*, retold by Roger Lancelyn Green
	From *King Arthur*, retold by Andrew Matthews and Peter Utton
Resources:	Big Book 5B pp. 8–12
	Pupil's Book 5 pp. 37–39
	Homework Book 5 p. 13: Homophones
	Copymaster 15: Different versions of the same story

Preparation

- (Optional) Collect different versions of the same traditional story for comparison.

DAY 1

Big Book 5B pp. 8–10; Pupil's Book pp. 37–38

Shared reading

- Discuss what the children already know of the story of King Arthur. How did they learn about him?

- Explain that a legend is a traditional story, about a heroic character, which may be based on truth, but which has been changed and added to down the years.

- Introduce them to this extract. We join the story just as Arthur draws the sword from the anvil in the stone to give it to Sir Kay. He is unaware at this time of the significance of what he has just done.

- Why does Sir Kay claim to be the true-born king of all Britain? Why does Sir Ector not believe him? What do the children think of Sir Kay?

- Ask the children to explain in their own words how Sir Ector discovered the truth.

- Compare the children's oral account with that of the story. What similarities and differences are there?

Focused word/sentence work

- Revise nouns. Ask the children to identify common and proper nouns in the text.

- Revise personal pronouns. Ask the children to identify some of those in the text and say to which nouns they refer: *it* – the sword; *him* – Sir Kay.

Independent work

- Children answer questions on the text.

Plenary

- Review the children's independent text work. Show them how to use the text to find literal answers, and how to use clues where information is not given directly.

DAY 2

Big Book 5B pp. 8–10; Pupil's Book p. 38

Shared reading

- Discuss the features of legends which this extract contains: a great hero, an amazing feat, its style of English. What other legends do the children know? In what ways are they similar to, or different from, the tale of King Arthur?

- Ask the children to read the story aloud, with a narrator and three children to read the words of Arthur, Sir Kay and Sir Ector.

Focused word/sentence work

- Identify examples of the style of language often used in legends, e.g. "Arthur knew nothing of what the sword was." How would we say such a sentence in everyday English?

- Discuss ways of changing selected sentences so that the meaning is retained.

Independent work

- Children construct sentences in different ways, while retaining meaning.

Plenary

- Review the children's sentence constructions. Discuss the changes and any effect on meaning. Compare the language of traditional stories (section C) with everyday English.

DAY 3

Big Book 5B pp. 8–10; Pupil's Book p. 39

Shared reading and writing, including focused word/sentence work

- Tell the children that they are going to write the story of Arthur for a younger audience. Ask them to decide who that audience will be: a younger brother or sister, other children in the school etc.

- Discuss how the story might be adapted for its intended reader. Ask the children to think about such things as vocabulary, sentence construction, and omitting or reducing detail.
- Identify words in the original text which younger children would find difficult, e.g. *anvil, scabbard, hilt, oath*. What words might be used instead? Might a different simile be used instead of "as if out of a greased scabbard"?
- Plan the story together in four paragraphs. Write the first paragraph to establish a suitable style.

Independent work
- Children begin writing their versions of the story of Arthur for a younger audience.

Plenary
- Review the work in progress. Encourage the children to evaluate their work.

DAY 4

Big Book 5B pp. 11–12; Pupil's Book p. 39

Shared reading
- Read the second version of the story of Arthur and the sword in the anvil.
- How is it similar to, or different from, the earlier version? Consider such things as style, vocabulary and detail.
- Ask the children to suggest reasons for the differences.
- Copymaster 15 gives guidance in investigating different versions of the same story.

Focused word/sentence work
- Compare the simile "as though the anvil had been carved out of black butter" with the previous "as if out of a greased scabbard". Which do the children prefer? Why? Can the children suggest a single word which might replace the simile, e.g. "easily"? Why is this much less effective? Discuss the differences between literal and figurative language.
- Ask the children to identify the adjectives in the final paragraph. Experiment with deleting them. How does this change the effect? Challenge the children to suggest alternative adjectives. How does this change the effect?

Independent work
- Children continue their writing.

Plenary
- Ask the children to read their stories aloud. Are they suitable for a younger audience? If not, what changes are needed?

DAY 5

Big Book 5B pp. 8–12; Pupil's Book p. 39

Shared reading
- Which version of the story do the children prefer? Ask them to give reasons for their answers.
- Read some of the children's stories out loud. How are they similar to, or different from, either of the two versions in this unit?

Focused word/sentence work
- Identify words in the passage which are homophones: words with the same pronunciation but different spellings, e.g. *vein/vain, red/read, to/too/two, know/no, read/reed, steal/steel*. Ask the children to tell you the corresponding homophone, to spell it, and to use it in a sentence of their own to show its meaning.
- Discuss other homophones, e.g. those in the previous version of the Arthur story: *rode/road, sent/scent, seen/scene, knight/night, see/sea, by/buy, hair/hare, forth/fourth*.

Independent work
- Children distinguish between homophones.

Plenary
- Review the children's work on homophones, re-emphasising teaching points and clarifying misconceptions.

Consolidation and extension
- Arrange with a teacher of younger children for your group to read their stories to the younger ones.
- Collect examples of traditional story vocabulary and sentence structure for the class to discuss.
- Make a collection of homophones, with sentences to show how they are used.
- Copymaster 15 gives guidance in investigating different versions of the same story.

Homework
- Page 13 in the Homework Book gives the children practice in distinguishing between homophones.

Unit 13

The Adventures of Rama and Sita

Key Learning Objectives

TL1	To identify and classify the features of myths, legends and fables
TL3	To explore similarities and differences between oral and written storytelling
TL8	To investigate narrative viewpoint and the treatment of different characters
TL14	To make notes of story outline as preparation for oral storytelling
SL4	To revise the different kinds of noun
SL6	To be aware of the differences between spoken and written language
SL7	To explore ambiguities that arise from sentence contractions
SL10	To ensure that, in using pronouns, it is clear to what or to whom they refer

Homophones?

Range:	Traditional story
Texts:	From *The Adventures of Rama and Sita*, retold by Ruskin Bond
Resources:	Big Book 5B pp. 13–17
	Pupil's Book 5 pp. 40–42
	Homework Book 5 p. 14: Nouns

Preparation

• The story of Rama and Sita is a favourite Diwali story. It is taken from an ancient Hindu poem, the *Ramayana*. It tells of how the god Vishnu came to earth to live as Prince Rama. He was the oldest son of a king, but Rama's wicked stepmother exiled him from the kingdom for 14 years so that her own son might become king instead. During this time Rama lived in a forest with his wife, Sita, and his brother Lakshman (or Lakshmana). Then one day Ravana, a demon, kidnapped Sita and carried her off to his island. Rama gathered an army of monkeys and went to rescue his wife. In battle he killed Ravana with a magic bow and arrow. When he returned home, people lit lamps to welcome him back as their king.

• Try to find a different version of this story to identify differences and similarities.

DAY 1

Big Book 5B pp. 13–15; Pupil's Book pp. 40–41

Shared reading

• Introduce the story to the children and read it together.

• Ask the children whether it is a myth, a fable or a legend. What makes them think so?

• Which character is this part of the story mainly about? Do the children think this is the main character in the story? What makes them think so/not? Who do they think the main character is? What makes them think so?

• If you have a different version of this story, read it to the children and compare the two. What differences are there? Why should this be? Discuss how and why stories change over time.

Focused word/sentence work

• Investigate selected words and phrases in the passage. What does the phrase "the tide of fortune" mean? Why does the author use the word "tide"? Ask the children to define and suggest synonyms for words in the text, e.g. *triumph, fray, source, roused, plight, cease, drowsy, ranks*. Which of the words are nouns, verbs or adjectives?

Independent work

• Children answer questions on the text.

Plenary

• Review the children's independent text work. Discuss and compare the features of legends, myths and fables.

DAY 2

Big Book 5B pp. 13–15; Pupil's Book p. 41

Shared reading

• Ask the children to read the story aloud.

• Ask them to retell the story in their own words. Compare the two versions, exploring the similarities between written and oral storytelling. You might choose to record the oral stories to make such a comparison easier.

Focused word/sentence work

• Revise nouns. Ask the children to pick out examples of common, proper and collective nouns from the text, e.g. *days, animals, Lakshman, Hanuman, armies*.

Independent work

• Children consolidate their understanding of common, proper and collective nouns.

Plenary

• Review the children's independent work on nouns, re-emphasising teaching points and clarifying misconceptions.

DAY 3

Big Book 5B pp. 13–15; Pupil's Book p. 42

Shared writing, including focused word/sentence work

• Discuss the differences between the text and the oral retelling on day 2. How great were the differences?

• How might making notes on the story help to prepare for a more detailed retelling? Demonstrate how to make notes. Identify the important words in the first paragraph. Show how names can be abbreviated. How might the names Rama and Ravana be abbreviated to avoid confusion?

• Ask the children to read the notes critically. Are they clear? Has anything important been missed out?

• Ask the children to use the notes to retell the first paragraph.

• Make clear that the children are to make their own notes on the extract as preparation for oral storytelling to the class.

Independent work

- Children begin writing notes on the story.

Plenary

- Review the children's notes, offering help and encouragement.

DAY 4

Big Book 5B pp. 16–17; Pupil's Book p. 42

Shared reading and writing

- Read the continuation of the story. Is this how the children expected the battle to end?
- As shared writing, make notes on this part of the story.
- Encourage the children to use the notes to retell the story.

Focused word/sentence work

- Ask the children to identify homophones in the text, e.g. *to/too/two, sent/scent, right/write, through/threw, their/there, one/won*. Encourage the children to distinguish between homophones, using them in sentences to show their meaning.
- Investigate the word "bow". How might this spelling be pronounced differently? How does this affect the meaning of the word? Discuss the homophones "bow" and "bough".

Independent work

- Children complete their notes, check them for completeness and clarity, and use them to prepare their oral storytelling.

Plenary

- Ask the children to retell the story to the class, using their notes to help them.

DAY 5

Big Book 5B pp. 13–17; Pupil's Book p. 42

Shared reading

- Read both parts of the story. Explore how the perspective of the story shifts from Lakshman to the Demon King, to his giant brother and finally to Rama as he kills Ravana with his magic arrows. Who are the heroes and villains in this story?
- Compare this story with a different genre, e.g. science fiction. In what ways are the two similar and different?

Focused word/sentence work

- Identify pronouns in the text, e.g. *he, his, himself, it*. Revise the function of pronouns.

- Look at the section *What does it really mean?* in the Pupil's Book. Why are some sentences ambiguous? How can they be made clearer? Discuss the importance of making clear to what or to whom pronouns refer.

Independent work

- Children explore ambiguity in the sentences in the Pupil's Book.

Plenary

- Discuss the possible meanings of the ambiguous sentences.
- Ask children to retell the story to the class, using their notes to help them.

Consolidation and extension

- Record the children's oral storytelling from notes. Compare this version with the earlier retelling without notes (see day 2). In what ways are the two versions different? Why? Why are written stories, even in note form, less likely to change than oral stories?
- Experiment with repeated oral retelling of the same story. Write a short story with lots of detail. Select six children to retell this story, but send four of them out of earshot. Read the story aloud to the class. Then ask the second child you selected to come back into the classroom. The first child now retells the story to him or her. The second child then retells the story to the third child and so on. As this continues, the rest of the children will begin to appreciate how stories change in the retelling. Compare the final oral version with the original written story. How has it changed? Why do the children think this happened?
- Ask the children to collect and classify different types of traditional story.
- Ask them to collect and classify different genres of story, e.g. science fiction, adventure. Discuss the similarities and differences.
- Challenge more able children to find examples of abstract nouns in the text, e.g. *joy, strength, freedom, fortune*. Ask them to use these nouns in sentences of their own.
- Explore ways of adapting oral storytelling to different audiences.

Homework

- Page 14 in the Homework Book gives further practice in classifying and using common, proper and collective nouns.

Unit 14 Fantastical Beasts

Key Learning Objectives

TL1 To identify and classify the features of myths, legends and fables

TL20 Note-making: to discuss what is meant by "in your own words" and when it is appropriate to copy, quote and adapt

TL21 To convert personal notes into notes for others to read, paying attention to appropriateness of style, vocabulary and presentation

TL22 To plan, compose, edit and refine short non-chronological reports, using reading as a source, focusing on clarity, conciseness, and impersonal style

TL24 To evaluate their work

SL4 To revise from Y4: the function of pronouns; agreement between pronouns and verbs

Range:	Non-chronological reports; Greek myth
Texts:	*Beasts from Myths and Legends* From *Giants and Warriors*, retold by James Reeves
Resources:	Big Book 5B pp. 18–21 Pupil's Book 5 pp. 43–45 Homework Book 5 p. 15: Relative pronouns Copymaster 16: Finding out: planning sheet Copymaster 17: Finding out: finding and recording information

Preparation

• From day 4 some children may be ready to find out about other fantastical beasts. To prepare for this make available suitable information books or IT sources, and have Copymasters 16 and 17 available.

DAY 1

Big Book 5B pp. 18–19; Pupil's Book pp. 43–44

Shared reading

• Have the children read or heard about any of these beasts before? Ask those who have to tell the rest of the class about them.

• Remind the children of the story of Odysseus and Polyphemus (see Collins *Focus on Literacy* Y3, Unit 19). What kind of person is Odysseus?

• Ask questions which give practice in scanning for information using headings, e.g. "How many heads does Cerberus have?"

• Ask questions which give practice in scanning for words and phrases, e.g. "Which creatures are half woman and half bird?"

• Practise searching for information from more than one source, e.g. "Which creatures have tails?"

Focused word/sentence work

• Ask the children to find words in the text which are homophones, e.g. *tail/tale, see/sea, hair/hare, turn/tern, maze/maize, sent/scent, to/too/two, no/know, one/won.*

What is the spelling of the corresponding homophones? Encourage the children to use them in sentences of their own.

Independent work

• Children answer questions about the text.

Plenary

• Review the children's independent text work. Check that the children can scan for information confidently and efficiently, and then are able to use close reading to aid understanding.

• Make sure they know how to compare and combine information from more than one source.

DAY 2

Big Book 5B pp. 18–19; Pupil's Book p. 44

Shared reading

• Ask the children to make up their own questions about the text for others to scan for the answers. Encourage them to identify the key words in the questions to aid the search.

• Discuss the range of fantastical beasts in legends and myths. How many of them are made from one or more creatures combined?

• Which creature seems the most frightening? Why?

• What other fantastical beasts do the children know from traditional stories? Ask them to describe these creatures, or tell their story.

Focused word/sentence work

• Revise personal pronouns from Y4: *I, me, you, he, she, it, we, us, you, they, them.*

• Ask the children to make up their own sentences using personal pronouns. Make sure the children understand the need for pronoun/verb agreement.

Independent work

• Children revise and consolidate the use of personal pronouns.

Plenary

• Make sure the children understand the function of personal pronouns and appreciate the aim to avoid needless and irritating repetition of nouns.

• Remind the children of the need to make clear to what or to whom pronouns refer (see Unit 13).

DAY 3

Big Book 5B pp. 18–19; Pupil's Book p. 45

Shared reading and writing, including focused word/sentence work

• Tell the children that they are going to make notes on the fantastical beasts, which they will subsequently use to write about them in their own words. Discuss what is meant by "in your own words".

• Choose one of the creatures described and pick out the most important words in the description. Write them as notes, showing the class how to use punctuation (commas, dashes, colons etc.) and abbreviations (e.g. P for Persia). Point out that when using an abbreviation its meaning must be clear, e.g. using P for Persia is only meaningful when the word occurs a second time.

- Read the notes through. Are they clear? Has anything important been missed out?

- Demonstrate how to reconstruct the notes into a non-chronological report using your own words to flesh them out. Point out that it is easier to do this if you do not look back at the original text. Emphasise that if the notes are carefully written and checked it should not be necessary to refer to the original.

- You may now choose to compare the two texts. How similar are they? Is your version truly in your own words? To what extent is this important? When is it appropriate to copy, quote and adapt?

Independent work

- Children begin writing their notes.

Plenary

- Review the children's notes, offering help and encouragement. Encourage them to evaluate their own work.

DAY 4

Big Book 5B pp. 20–21; Pupil's Book p. 45

Shared reading

- Read the extract from the story of Ariadne and Theseus. Note that further extracts in Unit 15 will tell how Theseus kills the Minotaur and escapes.

- Why do the children think Ariadne has given Theseus a ball of woollen thread? Remind them of where the Minotaur lives. How might Theseus use the thread?

- Ask the children to retell this part of the story in their own words.

Focused word/sentence work

- Investigate the use of commas in the text: when a person spoken to is addressed (*Handsome Athenian, I am grieved ...*); in direct speech (*"It is enchanted," she told him*); in embedding a clause in a sentence (*the monster, which is sacred, must have human victims*).

- Revise the use of other punctuation: speech marks, question marks, full stops.

- Investigate the spelling of "woollen".

Independent work

- Children complete their notes and use them to plan, compose, edit and refine non-chronological reports, paying attention to appropriateness of style, vocabulary and presentation.

- Some children may be ready to find out about the other fantastical beasts listed in the Pupil's Book. Make available suitable information books or IT sources. Copymasters 16 and 17 will help with this activity.

Plenary

- Review the children's notes and finished work. Discuss with the children how useful their notes were in helping them write their reports. What conclusions can they draw from this activity to help them in future note-making?

DAY 5

Big Book 5B pp. 20–21; Pupil's Book p. 45

Shared reading

- What features of Greek myths are to be found in this story?

- Investigate the traditional story language and style, e.g. "I am grieved", "it has been my unhappy lot", "to be slain". How is this different from everyday English? Experiment with constructing selected sentences in everyday English, while retaining meaning.

- Ask the children to read the story aloud. Choose three readers: Ariadne, Theseus and a narrator.

Focused word/sentence work

- Investigate the relative pronouns *who*, *whose* and *which*. Discuss how and when they are used, e.g. why do we use *which* when refering to the Minotaur, but *who* when referring to Ariadne or Theseus? In what context would we use the word *whose*?

- Ask the children to construct sentences using these relative pronouns.

Independent work

- Children consolidate their understanding of the relative pronouns *who*, *whose* and *which*.

Plenary

- Review the week's work, re-emphasising teaching points and clarifying misconceptions.

- Ask the children to read aloud some of their non-chronological reports on the fantastical beasts.

Consolidation and extension

- Ask the children to use books and IT sources to find out further information about the beasts described in the text.

- Make a class book of fantastical beasts, combining the reports written by the children using information from this unit and their own independent research.

- Make a computer database of this information.

- Copymaster 16 will help the children to prepare for reading by identifying what they already know and what they need to find out.

- Copymaster 17 will help the children to use indexes etc. to locate information confidently and efficiently, and to record sources.

- Encourage the children to make up their own fantastical beast, and to draw and write about it.

- Read to the children one or more Greek myths featuring mythological beasts.

Homework

- Page 15 in the Homework Book consolidates the work on the relative pronouns *who*, *whose* and *which*.

Unit 15 Theseus and the Minotaur

Key Learning Objectives

TL1	To identify and classify the features of myths, legends and fables
TL11	To write own versions of a Greek myth, using structures and themes identified in reading
TL13	To review and edit writing to produce a final form, matched to the needs of an identified reader
SL4	To revise from Y4 the function of pronouns
SL9	To secure the use of the comma in embedding clauses within sentences
WL7	To understand the correct use and spelling of possessive pronouns

Range:	Greek myth
Texts:	From *Giants and Warriors*, retold by James Reeves
Resources:	Big Book 5B pp. 22–25 Pupil's Book 5 pp. 46–48 Homework Book 5 p. 16: Possessive pronouns

DAY 1

Big Book 5B pp. 22–23; Pupil's Book pp. 46–47

Shared reading

- As preparation for this text, ask the children to retell in their own words the beginning of this story.
- What kind of traditional tale is this? How can the children tell?
- What extra information is given about the Minotaur in this story, compared with the description in Unit 14? How does the Minotaur attempt to kill Theseus?
- How does Theseus use the wool which Ariadne gave him? Is this what the children expected? What would the children do if they were in the labyrinth and the wool ran out before they found the Minotaur?
- Ask them to explain in their own words how Theseus killed the Minotaur.

Focused word/sentence work

- Explore the use of commas in the text: to signpost meaning in longer and more complex sentences, e.g. "Almost before he knew it, the creature was in front of him, scarcely a stone's throw away"; and also their use to embed clauses, e.g. "Once you have slain the Minotaur, you must find your way out of the maze."

Independent work

- Children answer questions on the text.

Plenary

- Review the children's independent text work. Discuss what the children think will happen next. Encourage them to justify their answers.

DAY 2

Big Book 5B pp. 22–23; Pupil's Book p. 47

Shared reading

- Who is the hero of this tale? Who is the villain? Is it the Minotaur or King Minos? Ask them to justify their answers.
- From whose point of view is this part of the story told?
- What do they think will happen next? How will Theseus and his companions get through the locked door of the labyrinth?
- Ask the children to retell the story as if they were Theseus relating his adventures to Ariadne.

Focused word/sentence work

- Ask the class to identify the word "its" in the text. How is it used? Discuss the difference between "its" and "it's".
- Investigate possessive pronouns: *mine, ours, yours, his, hers*. Discuss how they are used in sentences.

Independent work

- Children distinguish between "its" and "it's".
- Children investigate the function of possessive pronouns.

Plenary

- Review the children's independent work, re-emphasising teaching points and clarifying misconceptions. Make sure the children understand the difference between possessive pronouns and words which indicate possession: *my, our, your, his, her, its* and *their*, e.g. "this is your book", "this book is yours". In the second example the word "yours" stands in place of "your book" and so is a possessive pronoun.

DAY 3

Big Book 5B pp. 22–23; Pupil's Book p. 48

Shared reading/writing

- Discuss with the children ideas for their own story in the style of Theseus and the Minotaur. First select a monster. This may be one of those described in Unit 14, one from the children's own reading, or made up, e.g. with the body of a tiger, the head of a bull and the tail of a crocodile.
- Encourage them to invent a hero or a heroine, and perhaps a villain.
- Explore ideas for suitable settings, e.g. underground, a rocky mountain, a desert, a cave.
- What special weapons or other aids might the hero/heroine use? Where might he or she get them from?
- Plan the story in three or four paragraphs.

Focused word/sentence work

- Make a list of suitable words and phrases.

Independent work

- Children plan and begin writing their own story about a fantastical beast, in the style of a traditional story.

Plenary

- Review the work in progress, offering help and encouragement. How well are the stories planned? Discuss the effectiveness of the chosen characters and settings. Do the story openings make the reader want to read on?

DAY 4

Big Book 5B pp. 24–25; Pupil's Book p. 48

Shared reading

- Read the continuation of the story of Theseus. Is this how the children expected the story to continue?
- What lie might Ariadne have told to trick the key from the guards?
- What will King Minos do when he learns of the death of the sacred Minotaur and their escape?
- What further adventures might they have as they sail away?

Focused word/sentence work

- Revise the spelling pattern for adding *full* to a word, e.g. *successful*.
- Investigate antonyms for selected words in the text, e.g. *found, hurried, entrance, joy, return, triumph*.

Independent work

- Children continue their stories.

Plenary

- Review the children's stories. Encourage those who have finished a first draft to review and edit their writing.

DAY 5

Big Book 5B pp. 24–25; Pupil's Book p. 48

Shared reading

- Note how parallel action is related in stories, e.g. "While Theseus had been battling with the Minotaur, Ariadne ..."
- Who is the most important character in this part of the story? Why?
- Discuss Ariadne's role in saving the Greeks from the Minotaur.
- Ask the children to read aloud both extracts in this unit, using punctuation to help them with intonation and pauses.

Focused word/sentence work

- Discuss the difference between a phrase and a clause (a clause contains a verb).
- Investigate adjectival clauses beginning with *who, whose* or *which*. Give examples of such clauses as they are used in sentences. Ask the children to suggest others.
- Draw attention to how commas are used to embed clauses in sentences.

Independent work

- Children identify adjectival clauses in sentences, and make up their own, using commas to embed them in sentences.

Plenary

- Ask the children to read aloud some of their stories.
- Review the week's work on possessive pronouns and adjectival clauses. Re-emphasise teaching points and clarify misconceptions.

Consolidation and extension

- Ask the children to present their stories as a finished book with illustrations, a front cover with suitable artwork, and a back cover "blurb" introducing the story and its author.
- Encourage the children to find and read other versions of this Greek myth, and to compare them.
- Read other Greek myths to the children.
- Experiment with changing adjectives to adjectival clauses, e.g. the *happy* boy, the boy *who was happy*; the *injured* girl, the girl *who had a broken ankle*.
- Compare adjectival phrases with adjectival clauses, e.g. "the girl who had a broken ankle" (a clause containing the verb "had") and "with a broken ankle" (a phrase, as it has no verb).
- Ask the children to collect examples of possessive pronouns and adjectival clauses from their reading.

Homework

- Page 16 in the Homework Book consolidates work on possessive pronouns.

Unit 16 Myths

Key Learning Objectives

TL1   To identify and classify the features of myths

TL9   To investigate the features of different fiction genres, discussing the appeal of popular fiction

TL10   To understand the differences between literal and figurative language

TL11   To write own version of a myth, using structures and themes identified in reading

TL13   To review and edit writing to produce a final form, matched to the needs of an identified reader

TL24   To evaluate their work

SL1   To re-order simple sentences, noting the changes which are required in word order

SL8   To construct sentences in different ways, while retaining meaning

WL10 To investigate further antonyms; investigate common spelling patterns

WL12 To investigate metaphorical expressions

Range:	Myths
Texts:	From *West Indian Folk Tales*, retold by P. Sherlock
	From *How Stories Came into the World*, retold by Joanna Troughton
Resources:	Big Book 5B pp. 26–29
	Pupil's Book 5 pp. 49–51
	Homework Book 5 p. 17: Constructing sentences
	Copymaster 18: Exploring genre

DAY 1

Big Book 5B pp. 26–27; Pupil's Book pp. 49–50

Shared reading

- What typical features of a myth does this story have?
- What does this myth explain?
- Who does the class think Kabo Tano was? What makes them think so?
- Do the children think the Caribs stayed after cleaning up the Earth? What makes them think so?
- Did the children enjoy the story? Encourage them to give reasons for their answers.

Focused word/sentence work

- What do the children think "the bright procession of worlds" is? Discuss the metaphor. In what way is it a good description? Ask the children to identify and discuss another metaphor in the text, e.g. "the grey haze that carpeted the plains". How is this metaphor different from the simile "resting like a grey carpet"?
- Ask the children to pick out phrases they think are particularly effective descriptions, e.g. "the fires of sunrise".
- Discuss the differences between literal and figurative language.

Independent work

- Children answer questions on the text.

Plenary

- Review the children's independent text work. Discuss the children's opinions on the story.

DAY 2

Big Book 5B pp. 26–27; Pupil's Book p. 50

Shared reading

- Read the story again and then ask the children to tell the story in their own words. How is the retelling different from the written text?
- Note that this is a modern retelling of an old story. Why can we not read the original version?

Focused word/sentence work

- Explore antonyms. Pick out words from the text and ask the children to suggest opposites, e.g. *first*, *ancient*, *bright*. Which words have more than one antonym, e.g. *dull – bright, shining, sparkling, shimmering* etc. Discuss the difference between an antonym and a synonym.
- Explore words which do not have antonyms, e.g. *hair*, *green*, *cloud*.
- Investigate how some words can be made into antonyms by adding prefixes, e.g. *disobey, undo, unlike, dislike*.

Independent work

- Children explore antonyms, including those with more than one opposite, and those made by adding prefixes: *un-, dis-, im-, in-, non-* and *mis-*.

Plenary

- Review the children's work on antonyms. Discuss the variety of antonyms they have found in section B. How might a thesaurus be used to help with this work? Revise the difference between a synonym and an antonym.

DAY 3

Big Book 5B pp. 26–27; Pupil's Book p. 51

Shared writing

- Ask the children what the typical features of a myth are. Make a list. Tell the children that they are going to write their own myth giving a different explanation of who the first people were. How did they come to live on Earth? Where did they come from? What did they do? What happened then? Brainstorm ideas.
- Decide on an audience for the children's story. How might this affect the style and content? Discuss how the finished story is to be presented, e.g. as a book or a cassette.
- Plan the story in three or four paragraphs. Discuss ways of opening the story, perhaps using *The Caribs* as a model.

Focused word/sentence work

- Encourage the children to use descriptive language, including similes and metaphors, in the style of *The Caribs*.

Independent work

- Children plan and begin writing their own myth explaining how the first people came to live on the Earth.

Plenary

- Review the work in progress. Encourage the children to review their own work.

DAY 4

Big Book 5B pp. 28–29; Pupil's Book p. 51

Shared reading

- Read the myth *Thunder and Lightning*. What typical features of a myth does this story have? In what ways is it similar to and different from *The Caribs*?
- Ask the children to explain how the behaviour of Thunder and Lightning is like real thunder and lightning.
- How does this story explain why we see lightning before we hear thunder?

Focused word/sentence work

- Investigate antonyms for words in the text, e.g. *old, far, possible*. Ask the children to use the antonyms in sentences.
- Explore synonyms for selected words, e.g. *old, complain, harm*.
- What is the difference in meaning between "lightning" and "lightening"?

Independent work

- Children continue writing their own myths.

Plenary

- Review the children's writing. Encourage the children to review and edit their writing.

DAY 5

Big Book 5B pp. 26–29; Pupil's Book p. 51

Shared reading

- Investigate the style of the two stories. Which story is intended for a younger audience? How can the children tell?
- Use Copymaster 18 to explore this particular story genre. Note that this sheet may be used to explore any genre with which the children are familiar.

Focused word/sentence work

- Experiment with re-ordering selected sentences. Which changes require changes of verb form? Discuss the effects on meaning.
- Experiment with deleting words to retain the basic meaning of the sentence.

Independent work

- Children experiment with constructing sentences: changing word order to retain meaning, deleting words to shorten a sentence, and adding words to simple sentences to make them more interesting.

Plenary

- Review the children's sentence constructions. Draw attention to the need to use commas when embedding clauses.
- Encourage the children to evaluate their own myths.

Consolidation and extension

- Make a class book of antonyms, each word on an opposite page to its antonym. For each word, ask the children to supply a definition, a sentence showing how it is used, and an amusing illustration.
- Collect a selection of myths which explain natural phenomena. Compare them. Which do the children like best? Why?
- Copymaster 18 encourages the children to explore genre, commenting on settings, characters, plot and language. Use this sheet when the children have read a few stories within a single genre. The Copymaster may be used again for different genres.

Homework

- Page 17 in the Homework Book gives practice in rewriting sentences to change and retain meaning, and also in expanding simple sentences using clauses and phrases with appropriate punctuation.

Unit 17 Rain, Thunder and Lightning

Key Learning Objectives

TL15 To read explanatory texts, investigating and noting features of impersonal style

TL16 To prepare for reading by identifying what they already know and what they need to find out

TL17 To locate information confidently and efficiently

TL18 To know how authors record and acknowledge their sources

TL19 To evaluate texts critically by comparing how different sources treat the same information

TL20 Note-making: to discuss what is meant by "in your own words" and when it is appropriate to copy, quote and adapt

TL22 To plan, compose, edit and refine a short explanatory text, using reading as a source, focusing on clarity, conciseness, and impersonal style

TL23 To record and acknowledge sources in their own writing

TL24 To evaluate their work

SL1 To re-order simple sentences, noting the changes which are required in word order and verb forms, and discuss the effects of changes

SL5 To use punctuation effectively to signpost meaning in longer and more complex sentences

SL8 To construct sentences in different ways, while retaining meaning

SL9 To secure the use of the comma in embedding clauses within sentences

WL4 To explore spelling patterns of consonants and to formulate rules

WL9 To search for, collect, define and spell technical words derived from work in other subjects

Range:	Explanations
Texts:	*Rain, Thunder and Lightning*
Resources:	Big Book 5B pp. 30–33
	Pupil's Book 5 pp. 52–54
	Homework Book 5 p. 18: Joining sentences
	Copymaster 19: A glossary of terms
	Copymaster 20: Comparing information texts

Preparation

- The children will need access to a range of information books or IT sources from day 4 for researching processes from a range of subject areas.

DAY 1

Big Book 5B pp. 30–31; Pupil's Book pp. 52–53

Shared reading

- Read the text and study the illustration. To what extent does the illustration help the children understand the text?
- Ask the children to explain the water cycle in their own words.

Focused word/sentence work

- Explore the spelling patterns of consonants and revise the rules: *ll* in *full* becomes *l* when used as a suffix, e.g. *harmful, useful*; words ending in a short vowel double the consonant before adding a suffix, e.g. *bigger*. Note that *c* is soft in the word "process", as is the first *c* in "cycle".
- Ask the children to suggest other words with these patterns.

Independent work

- Children answer questions about the water cycle.

Plenary

- Review the children's independent text work. Ask them to explain why water can never be used up completely.

DAY 2

Big Book 5B pp. 30–31; Pupil's Book p. 53

Shared reading

- Investigate the features of impersonal style in this explanatory text, e.g. complex sentences, passive voice, technical vocabulary, hypothetical language (*if* the clouds become cold enough *then* ...), use of words and phrases to make sequential, causal, logical connections (*only after, at the same time, when, causes, so that*).

Focused word/sentence work

- Ask the children to experiment with expressing selected sentences from the text in a different way, while retaining meaning, e.g. by re-ordering them or by deleting or substituting words.
- Discuss the effects of the changes.

Independent work

- Children construct sentences to express the same idea in a different way.

Plenary

- Review the children's sentence constructions. Do they express the same idea as the original? If not, why not? Are they properly punctuated? How many different ways of expressing the same idea are there?

DAY 3

Big Book 5B pp. 30–31; Pupil's Book p. 54

Shared reading/writing, including focused word/sentence work

- Read again the part of the text which describes the water purification process. Make notes. Evaluate them for clarity and conciseness. Plan how to use them to write an explanatory text in your own words.
- Focus on the features of impersonal style appropriate to this kind of writing.

Independent work

- Children write notes on water purification and use them to write a short explanatory text.

Plenary

- Review the work in progress. Encourage the children to edit and refine their notes and explanations.

DAY 4

Big Book 5B pp. 32–33; Pupil's Book p. 54

Shared reading

- Compare the real explanation of thunder and lightning with the myth *Thunder and Lightning* in Unit 16. Why did ancient peoples not know the true explanation? Why did they need a story which seems to explain it? How might the true explanation be known today?
- Ask the children to explain the difference between sheet lightning and fork lightning. Which kind is the more dangerous? Why?
- Ask the children to explain in their own words the cause of thunder.

Focused word/sentence work

- Ask the children to identify the technical words in the text. Make a list and encourage them to suggest definitions, checking these with a suitable dictionary.
- Copymaster 19 encourages the children to collect and define technical words from their reading and own interests.

Independent work

- Children begin research on a process selected from the list in the Pupil's Book. They then make notes on the process for their own explanatory text. Time will be required outside the literacy hour to continue and complete this task.
- Copymasters 16 and 17 will prove useful here, encouraging the children to prepare for reading, to locate information confidently and efficiently, and to record and acknowledge their sources.

Plenary

- Encourage the children to evaluate the texts they are researching, critically comparing how different sources treat the same information.
- Copymaster 20 will help with this comparison.
- Use selected books to show the children how authors record and acknowledge their sources.

DAY 5

Big Book 5B pp. 32–33; Pupil's Book p. 54

Shared reading

- Investigate the features of impersonal style in this explanatory text, e.g. complex sentences, passive voice, technical vocabulary, use of words and phrases to make sequential, causal, logical connections (*as, eventually, such that, so that, because*).
- Ask the children to explain, in their own words, how to work out roughly how far away a thunderstorm is.

Focused word/sentence work

- Investigate longer and more complex sentences in the text. Break selected ones down into sentences expressing single ideas, to show how they have been constructed.
- Experiment with combining these in different ways to construct longer sentences which express the same idea as those in the text. Identify the conjunctions used to do this.

Independent work

- Children construct sentences by combining two others using a variety of conjunctions.
- Show them how to record and acknowledge sources in their own writing.

Plenary

- Review the children's work on explanatory texts. Encourage them to evaluate their own work, focusing on clarity, conciseness and impersonal style.

Consolidation and extension

- Children complete their research, notes and explanatory texts, editing and refining them.
- Encourage the children to evaluate their work, focusing on clarity, conciseness and impersonal style.
- Copymaster 19 encourages the children to collect and define technical words from their reading and own interests.
- Copymaster 20 helps the children compare how different texts treat the same information.

Homework

- Page 18 in the Homework Book gives further practice in joining sentences with a variety of conjunctions.

Unit 18 Bishop Hatto

Key Learning Objectives

TL4	To read a range of narrative poems
TL5	To perform poems in a variety of ways
TL6	To understand terms which describe different kinds of poem and identify typical features
TL7	To compile a class anthology of favourite poems with commentaries which illuminate choice
TL10	To understand the differences between literal and figurative language
TL12	To use the structures of poems read, to write extensions based on these
WL5	To investigate words which have common letter strings but different pronunciations
WL10	To investigate further antonyms; investigate common spelling patterns and other ways of creating opposites through additional words and phrases

Range:	Longer, classic, narrative poem
Text:	*Bishop Hatto*, Robert Southey
Resources:	Big Book 5B pp. 34–38 Pupil's Book 5 pp. 55–58 Homework Book 5 p. 19: Investigating words

Preparation

- Note that there is a single text in this unit, the poem *Bishop Hatto*. The notes below assume that the whole poem will be read on day 1.

DAY 1

Big Book 5B pp. 34–38; Pupil's Book pp. 55–57

Shared reading

- Robert Southey's poem is based on the story of Bishop Hatto, a 10th-century archbishop of Mainz. It is said that in a time of famine, in order that there might be more for the rich, he assembled the poor in a barn and burned them to death. He said, "They are like mice. Only good to devour corn." Soon an army of mice caused him to retreat to his tower on the Rhine, where the mice devoured him. The tower is still known as the Mouse Tower. In Southey's poem the rodents are rats.

- Discuss the events of the story. Why did the bishop burn the barn? What do the children think of this action?

- Why do the children think Southey put rats instead of mice in his story? Are rats more frightening than mice? Why?

- Did the class enjoy reading the story? Why?

Focused word/sentence work

- Ask the children to find examples of old-fashioned language and punctuation. Why are some common nouns given capital letters, e.g. Rats? What is the missing letter in words such as "furnish'd"? Why is the letter missed out? (Often, in older poems, the word "furnished" might have three syllables. The apostrophe indicates to the reader that "furnish'd" is a two-syllable word.)

- What do words such as *'twas*, *'tis*, *i'faith*, and *quoth* mean?

Independent work

- Children answer questions on the poem.

Plenary

- Discuss the children's answers to the comprehension. How did the poem make them feel? Which lines or verses made them feel that way?

DAY 2

Big Book 5B pp. 34–38; Pupil's Book p. 57

Shared reading

- What kind of poem is this? Discuss what makes a narrative poem. What are the features of a ballad? (A poem which tells a story, and usually has short, regular verses with line endings which rhyme.)

- What rhyming pattern does this poem have?

- Which verse breaks the four-line pattern in this poem? Ask the children to suggest reasons for this. What rhyming pattern does this verse have?

- Which parts of the poem did the children find the most frightening? Why? Which words and phrases made them feel that way?

Focused word/sentence work

- Identify words in the poem such as "good", "food" and "floor", which have common letter strings but different pronunciations.

- Collect similar letter strings, e.g. *ea* in "great", "sweat", "scream"; *ou* in "young", "ground", "pour"; *all* in "hall" and "shall"; *or* in "for" and "work"; *ei* in "ceiling" and "rein".

Independent work

- Children investigate words which have identical letter strings but different pronunciations.

Plenary

- Review the children's independent work, re-emphasising teaching points and clarifying misconceptions.

DAY 3

Big Book 5B pp. 34–38; Pupil's Book p. 58

Shared reading/writing, including focused word/sentence work

- Identify examples of figurative language, e.g. "eyes of flame", "an army of rats". Why are these powerful expressions? What different pictures do the expressions "army of rats" and "ten thousand rats" make? What special effect does the word "army" have?

- Identify examples of literal imagery, e.g. "through the walls helter-skelter they pour". Discuss the difference between literal and figurative language.
- Which verses are particularly effective? Why?
- Discuss the ideas in the Pupil's Book for a new verse for the poem. Brainstorm ideas. Encourage vivid imagery using figurative or literal language. Write down suitable words and phrases. Work out ways of expressing these ideas in a four-line verse with an AABB rhyming pattern.

Independent work

- Children write their own new verse for the *Bishop Hatto* poem.

Plenary

- Review the children's work. How well do their verses fit the structure and style of the original poem? Which work best? Why?

DAY 4

Big Book 5B pp. 34–38; Pupil's Book p. 58

Shared reading

- Discuss ways of performing the poem with groups reading different parts of the poem, and single voices for the bishop and the man from the farm.
- Experiment with different approaches. Record a variety of readings on tape for later evaluation.

Focused word/sentence work

- Find other words which have homophones, e.g. *great, there, eye, sent, told, yore, through, right*. What are the corresponding homophones for these words?
- Ask the children to put them in sentences to show how they are used.

Independent work

- Children rewrite selected verses from the poem with new words and/or ideas.

Plenary

- Review the children's verses. Which does the class like best? Why?

DAY 5

Big Book 5B pp. 34–38; Pupil's Book p. 58

Shared reading

- Review the recordings from day 4. Decide on the most effective way to perform the poem.
- Record the performance on tape.
- Review the performance. Discuss possible improvements.
- Perform the poem again, incorporating the improvements.

Focused word/sentence work

- Ask the children to find antonyms for selected words in the poem, e.g. *wet, lie, poor, plentiful*.
- Investigate phrases which are the opposites to these words, e.g. *plentiful* – not enough, *poor* – having lots of money.

Independent work

- Children make further investigations into antonyms, including ways of creating antonym-style phrases.

Plenary

- Review the children's work on antonyms, re-emphasising teaching points and clarifying misconceptions.

Consolidation and extension

- Perform the poem to another class, or the rest of the school.
- Compile a class anthology of favourite poems. Ask the children to write commentaries on the poems, saying what they like about them and what their main features are.
- Make a collection of words with common letter strings but different pronunciations. Which letter strings have the most different pronunciations?

Homework

- Page 19 in the Homework Book encourages the children to investigate words through definitions, synonyms and antonyms.

Unit 19 Cautionary Tales

Key Learning Objectives

TL4	To read a range of narrative poems
TL5	To perform poems in a variety of ways
TL10	To understand the differences between literal and figurative language
TL12	To use the structures of poems read, to write extensions based on these
SL2	To consolidate the basic conventions of standard English
SL7	To explore ambiguities that arise from sentence contractions
WL8	To recognise and spell the suffixes *-cian, -tion, -ous, -ment, -ship*

Range:	Longer, classic, narrative poem Modern cautionary tale
Texts:	*Matilda*, Hilaire Belloc From *The Boy Who Cried Wolf*, Tony Ross
Resources:	Big Book 5B pp. 39–43 Pupil's Book 5 pp. 59–62 Homework Book 5 p. 20: Correcting sentences

DAY 1

Big Book 5B pp. 39–41; Pupil's Book pp. 59–60

Shared reading

- In what way is this cautionary tale like a fable? In what way is it different? What is the moral of the story?
- What kind of poem is it? How can you tell?
- How is this poem different from *Bishop Hatto* in Unit 18?
- How does the poem make the children feel? Why?
- Which lines do the children like best? Why?

Focused word/sentence work

- Investigate punctuation in the poem: commas, semi-colons, exclamation marks, speech marks, dashes, brackets, capital letters.

Independent work

- Children answer questions on the poem.

Plenary

- Review the children's answers. Discuss the children's favourite lines from the poem. Ask the children to justify their preferences.

DAY 2

Big Book 5B pp. 39–41; Pupil's Book pp. 59–60

Shared reading

- What is the rhyming pattern?
- What is the main idea of each verse?
- How can we tell that the firemen were enthusiastic when they came to the house?
- What effect did Matilda's lies have on people? What effect did her lies have on her aunt? How did the people in the street react to her shout of "Fire"? Why?
- What do you think "this infirmity" (line 8) refers to?
- Point out the alliteration in "tiptoe to the telephone".

Focused word/sentence work

- Investigate suffixes in the poem, e.g. dread*ful*, earli*est*, infirm*ity*, frenz*ied*, depriv*ation*. What are the root words? How does the suffix affect meaning?
- Investigate the suffixes *-cian, -tion, -ous, -ment* and *-ship*.

Independent work

- Children investigate the suffixes *-cian, -tion, -ous, -ment* and *-ship*.

Plenary

- Review the children's work on suffixes. Ask them to put the words they have made in sentences to show their meaning.

DAY 3

Big Book 5B pp. 39–43; Pupil's Book pp. 61–62

Shared reading and writing

- Read the second text, *The Boy Who Cried Wolf*. In what ways is it similar to the story of Matilda? In what ways is it different?
- Plan together a new cautionary tale using one of the suggestions in the Pupil's Book, or an idea arising from discussion.
- Decide whether to write it as a narrative poem, using the structure of *Matilda*, or as a story in the manner of *The Boy Who Cried Wolf*.
- Plan the story along the lines suggested in the Pupil's Book.

Focused word/sentence work

- Revise the use of speech marks and exclamation marks.

Independent work

- Children begin writing their cautionary tales.

Plenary

- Review the children's writing in progress, offering help and encouragement.

DAY 4

Big Book 5B pp. 39–43; Pupil's Book pp. 59–62

Shared reading

- Why did Matilda call the fire brigade? (She was bored.) Why did Harry cry "Wolf!"? (To avoid doing things he hated.) Who seems the naughtier child? Why?
- How do the children think the story will end? What makes them think so?
- Which do the children think is older, the story or the poem? Ask them to justify their answers.
- One of the two is written for young children. Which does the class think this is? Why?

Focused word/sentence work

- Ask the children to experiment with changing the word order in selected sentences. Discuss the effect of the changes on meaning, verb form and punctuation.

Independent work

- Children continue their cautionary tales.

Plenary

- Review the children's cautionary tales. Encourage them to review and edit their work to produce a final form.

DAY 5

Big Book 5B pp. 39–41; Pupil's Book p. 62

Shared reading

- Experiment with ways of performing the poem. It may be read as choral speech, perhaps with some children miming the action, e.g. gasping and stretching eyes, tiptoeing to the telephone, the arrival of the firemen, the crowd cheering etc.
- Record the performance on video or audio tape for evaluation.

Focused word/sentence work

- Investigate how the punctuation helps with reading the poem aloud.

Independent work

- Children explore ambiguity in sentences and sentence contractions.

Plenary

- Review the children's work on ambiguity.

Consolidation and extension

- Perform the poem to another class, or to the rest of the school.
- Make a cartoon strip of the poem.
- Collect other examples of cautionary tales, especially poems by Hilaire Belloc. What aspect do they have in common?
- Make a collection of ambiguities from signs and headlines.
- Collect further examples of words with suffixes. Identify the root word and discuss the effect of adding the suffix.

Homework

- Page 20 in the Homework Book consolidates understanding of the basic conventions of standard English.

Unit 20   Traditional Tales

Key Learning Objectives

TL2	To investigate different versions of the same story in print or on film, identifying similarities and differences; recognise how stories change over time, and differences of culture and place that are expressed in stories
TL3	To explore similarities and differences between oral and written storytelling
TL8	To distinguish between the author and the narrator, investigating narrative viewpoint and the treatment of different characters
TL11	To write own version of a traditional story, using structures and themes identified in reading
TL13	To review and edit writing to produce a final form, matched to the needs of an identified reader
TL24	To evaluate their work
SL5	To use punctuation effectively to signpost meaning in longer and more complex sentences
SL9	To secure the use of the comma in embedding clauses within sentences
WL12	To investigate metaphorical expressions and figures of speech from everyday life

Range:	Traditional stories
Texts:	From *The Tale of Ali Baba and the Forty Thieves*, translated by Anthea Bell From *Turkish Folk-Tales*, retold by Barbara K. Walker
Resources:	Big Book 5B pp. 44–48 Pupil's Book 5 pp. 63–66 Homework Book 5 p. 21: Everyday expressions Copymaster 21: Book review Copymaster 22: Revision – term 2 assessment master

Preparation

- Make available one or more different versions of the story of Ali Baba, in print or on film.

DAY 1

Big Book 5B pp. 44–46; Pupil's Book pp. 63–64

Shared reading

- Read the story of Ali Baba. Discuss why Ali Baba behaved in the way he did.
- What risks did he take in entering the cave?
- Compare the version here with another version of the same story. How are they different? How are they similar? Ask the children to suggest reasons for these differences.

Focused word/sentence work

- Challenge the children to find synonyms and antonyms for selected words in the text, e.g. *large, approaching, fast, armed.*

Independent work

- Children answer questions on the story of Ali Baba.

Plenary

- Review the children's independent text work. Discuss the children's opinions of Ali Baba.

DAY 2

Big Book 5B pp. 44–46; Pupil's Book p. 64

Shared reading

- What clues are there that this is a traditional story set in a distant place and time?
- From whose point of view is the story told? How would it differ if it were told from the point of view of the captain of the robbers? What important things would be left out? What would we then be told that Ali Baba was unable to see?
- Who is the narrator? Would the story change much if Ali Baba were the narrator? Why not?

Focused word/sentence work

- Look at selected complex sentences in the text. Pick out the subordinate clauses, e.g. "while he was at work cutting down trees". Remind the children that a clause is a group of words with a verb.
- Investigate the first sentence in the text. What is the main clause? ("Ali Baba saw a large cloud of dust.") Ask the children to identify the two subordinate clauses which support this main idea and the phrase "one day" which tells us when the action happened.
- Encourage the children to make complex sentences from simple sentences by adding a clause, e.g. "Ali Baba was a poor man, *who lived in Persia.*"

Independent work

- Children explore clauses.

Plenary

- Review the children's work on clauses. Discuss where commas are needed to embed the clauses in sentences.

DAY 3

Big Book 5B pp. 44–48; Pupil's Book pp. 65–66

Shared reading and writing, including focused word/sentence work

- Read the second traditional story *I Know What I'll Do.*
- Playing tricks is a typical theme of many traditional stories. Ask the children to explain how the Hoca tricks the tricksters into bringing back his bag.
- Discuss the ideas in the Pupil's Book for writing a "traditional" story. Select one for the shared writing. Brainstorm ideas. Discuss for whom the story is to be written. Talk about setting and characters. From whose point of view is the story to be told? Will it be written in the first or third person?

- Plan the story in three or four paragraphs. Decide on a good opening sentence, beginning as these stories do with the phrase "one day".

- Write the first paragraph together. Show how to build complex sentences by embedding clauses.

Independent work

- Children plan and begin writing their own traditional story based on either *Ali Baba* or *I Know What I'll Do*.

Plenary

- Review the children's writing, offering help and encouragement. Draw the children's attention to effective use of subordinate clauses.

DAY 4

Big Book 5B pp. 47–48; Pupil's Book p. 66

Shared reading

- Before you read *I Know What I'll Do* again, ask the children whether they can identify from whose point of view the story is being told.

- Note that the story is not really told from the point of view of either the Hoca or his students. The author gives us a "god's eye view" of events. We see what the boys do when the Hoca is not watching, and what he does when his students are not there. What would be missed out if the story were told from only the Hoca's point of view or from that of the boys?

- How does the author make us feel about the characters?

Focused word/sentence work

- What do the children think "hoca" means? What clues to meaning are there in the story?

- Revise pronouns and nouns. Ask the children to identify examples of each. Which nouns are abstract nouns (e.g. *astonishment, curiosity*)?

- Ask the children to identify the use of commas in the text to signpost meaning.

Independent work

- Children continue their traditional stories.

Plenary

- Ask some of the children who have finished writing to read their stories aloud.

- Encourage the class to review and edit their work to produce a final form, matched to the needs of their audience.

DAY 5

Big Book 5B pp. 47–48; Pupil's Book p. 66

Shared reading

- What kind of man is the Hoca? Ask the children to justify their answers.

- Which story do the children like best? Why?

- Ask those who know the tale of Ali Baba to retell the story in the Big Book and then to say what happens next.

- How is the children's own version different from the written story? How is it similar?

Focused word/sentence work

- Discuss the meaning of metaphorical expressions and figures of speech from everyday life. In the story, the Hoca's students try to *pull his leg*, but the Hoca *smells a rat* and *turns the tables* on them. The students take the saddlebag *for a lark*, but the Hoca *pays them back in their own coin*.

- Brainstorm other such expressions and ask the children to explain them.

Independent work

- Children investigate metaphorical expressions and figures of speech from everyday life.

Plenary

- Review the week's work, re-emphasising teaching points and clarifying misconceptions.

Consolidation and extension

- Collect everyday expressions. Make a book explaining them, illustrated with amusing pictures.

- Challenge the children to expand a simple sentence by adding a clause, each child providing a different clause for the same main clause. Compare and classify their suggestions.

- Act out an improvised version of one or both stories.

- Use suitable expressions as titles for stories in traditional style, e.g. *playing with fire, from pillar to post*.

- Copymaster 21 is a book review focusing on narrative viewpoint and the treatment of different characters.

Homework

- Page 21 in the Homework Book investigates further metaphorical expressions and figures of speech from everyday life.

ASSESSMENT

Copymaster 22 is an assessment master of key word and sentence objectives for term 2, testing the children's ability to: distinguish between homophones; join sentences in a variety of ways; embed clauses in sentences using appropriate punctuation; change simple sentences into complex sentences. Indirectly, it will also test vocabulary, spelling and handwriting. The completed sheet will be useful as a record of progress, together with examples of the pupil's text work.

HALF TERMLY PLANNER

Year 5 • Term 3 • Weeks 1–5

SCHOOL _____ **CLASS** _____ **TEACHER** _____

		Phonetics, spelling and vocabulary	Grammar and punctuation	Comprehension and composition	Texts
Continuous work **Weeks 1–5**		WL 1, 2, 3	SL 1		**Range** **Fiction and poetry:** novels and stories from a variety of cultures and traditions **Non-fiction:** persuasive writing to put or argue a point of view: letters, commentaries to persuade, protest, object, complain; dictionaries, thesauruses, including IT sources
Blocked work **Week**	**Unit**				**Titles**
1	21	WL 4, 5, 6, 8	SL 3	TL 1, 2, 8, 9	From *Trust You Wriggly*, Grace Nichols From *The Mystery of the House of Pigeons*, Subhadra Sengupta
2	22	WL 5, 7, 12	SL 5	TL 1, 2, 3, 7, 10	From *Getting Granny's Glasses*, Ruskin Bond
3	23		SL 4, 6, 7	TL 1, 2, 3, 7, 9	From *The Banana Machine*, Alexander McCall Smith
4	24	WL 5, 11, 12, 13	SL 4, 6, 7	TL 1, 2, 3, 9	From *Akimbo and the Crocodile Man*, Alexander McCall Smith
5	25	WL 12		TL 12, 13, 14, 15, 17	Newspaper cuttings Dear BBC, from *Young Letter Writers*, letters chosen by the Royal Mail

SCHOOL _____ CLASS _____ TEACHER _____

		Phonetics, spelling and vocabulary	Grammar and punctuation	Comprehension and composition	Texts
Continuous work **Weeks 6–10**		WL 1, 2, 3	SL 1		**Range** **Fiction and poetry**: novels, stories and poems from a variety of cultures and traditions; choral and performance poetry **Non-fiction**: persuasive writing to put or argue a point of view; commentaries to persuade, protest, support
Blocked work					
Week	**Unit**				**Titles**
6	26	WL 4, 13	SL 2	TL 14, 15, 16, 19	From *The Blue Peter Green Book*, Lewis Bronze, Nick Heathcote and Peter Brown From *Earth Alert*, James Marsh
7	27	WL 5, 10		TL 14, 15, 16, 18	From *The Blue Peter Green Book*, Lewis Bronze, Nick Heathcote and Peter Brown From *Protecting Endangered Species*, Felicity Brooks
8	28	WL 6, 9, 13		TL 4, 5, 11	*The Ceremonial Band*, James Reeves; *The Pow-wow Drum*, David Campbell; *Rap Connected*, Benjamin Zephaniah
9	29		SL 5	TL 4, 11	*Night Mail*, W.H. Auden; *From a Railway Carriage*, Robert Louis Stevenson
10	30		SL 1, 2, 4, 6, 7	TL 2, 3, 6, 9	From *The Borrowers Afield*, Mary Norton

Unit 21 Moonlight and Candlelight

Key Learning Objectives

TL1   To investigate a range of texts from different cultures, considering patterns of attitudes and beliefs

TL2   To identify the point of view from which a story is told and how this affects the reader's response

TL8   To record predictions, questions, reflections while reading

TL9   To write in the style of the author

SL3   To search for, identify and classify a range of prepositions; experiment with substituting different prepositions and their effect on meaning; Understand and use the term *preposition*

WL4   To spell unstressed vowels in polysyllabic words

WL5   To investigate and learn spelling rules: words ending in *e* drop *e* when adding *-ing*

WL6   To transform words by changing tenses: *-e, -ing*

WL8   To identify everyday words which have been borrowed from other languages and to understand how this might give clues to spelling

Range:	Novels, stories from a variety of cultures and traditions
Texts:	From *Trust You Wriggly*, Grace Nichols From *The Mystery of the House of Pigeons*, Subhadra Sengupta
Resources:	Big Book 5C pp. 4–7 Pupil's Book 5 pp. 67–69 Homework Book 5 p. 22: Prepositions Copymaster 23: Reading journal Copymaster 24: Words borrowed from other languages

DAY 1

Big Book 5C pp. 4–5; Pupil's Book pp. 67–68

Shared reading

- What clues are there that this story is set in Guyana?

- From whose point of view is the story told? Explore Wriggly's changing thoughts and feelings as the story unfolds. What prompts these changes?

- What sort of person do the children think Wriggly is? What makes them think so?

Focused word/sentence work

- Look at the words which are unfamiliar to most children, but everyday words in Guyana: "puzzling-tin", "vine-rope", "courida". What do the children think these might be? What makes them think so?

- Pick out polysyllabic words with unstressed vowels, e.g. fin**a**lly, sil**e**nce, mom**e**nt, heav**e**n. Discuss the spelling.

- Investigate the comparative endings in "pink*ish*" and "fast*er*".

Independent work

- Children answer questions on the text.

Plenary

- Review the children's independent text work. Discuss the children's reflections on Wriggly and how she might react later in the story.

DAY 2

Big Book 5C pp. 4–5; Pupil's Book pp. 67–68

Shared reading

- Encourage the children to reflect on Wriggly's actions, thoughts and feelings. Why should Wriggly feel so strongly that the world is about to end? Discuss the events which contribute to this fear.

- How would the class have felt in a similar situation? To what extent would they feel the same? How might they feel differently? Discuss the reasons for these differences.

- Enourage the children to keep a reading journal, to record predictions, questions and reflections while reading. Use Copymaster 23 for this activity.

Focused word/sentence work

- Explain the term "preposition". Ask the children to search for and identify prepositions in the text, e.g. *in, around, from, on, down, between*.

- Discuss their meanings.

Independent work

- Children investigate prepositions.

Plenary

- Review the children's work on prepositions. Discuss the effect on meaning of the substituted prepositions in section B in the Pupil's Book.

DAY 3

Big Book 5C pp. 4–5; Pupil's Book p. 69

Shared reading and writing

- How might the coin Wriggly found influence future events?

- What might Wriggly do now? What makes the children think so?

- Plan a story about what happens next. Write a first paragraph together in the style of Grace Nichols.

Focused word/sentence work

- Note Grace Nichols' use of longer complex sentences and short simple ones.

- Note the range of connectives she uses to link clauses within sentences, e.g. *and finally, as, when, until*.

Independent work

- Children begin writing further events in the story of Wriggly, using the style of the author.

Plenary

- Review the work in progress. Compare the style of the children's writing with that of the author, Grace Nichols.

DAY 4

Big Book 5C pp. 6–7; Pupil's Book p. 69

Shared reading

- What clues are there that this story is set in a foreign land? Which land do the children think this might be? What makes them think so?
- What customs and beliefs does the text refer to? How is Diwali similar to celebrations the children are familiar with? Encourage them to refer to the text when answering.
- From whose point of view is the story told?

Focused word/sentence work

- Why are certain words in the text printed in italics?
- Investigate words in the text which have been borrowed from other languages. Discuss their spelling.
- The words *halva* (Turkish) and *puri* (Hindi) appear in several English dictionaries, but *ladoos*, *barfi*, *sewaiyan* and *galis* have not yet been "borrowed". The word *veranda* (sometimes spelt *verandah*) has been borrowed from the Hindi word *varanda*. *Garland* comes from the old French *garlande*. *Rocket* derives from the Italian *rocchetta*.

Independent work

- Children continue their writing.

Plenary

- Ask the children to read their stories aloud. Are the actions, thoughts and feelings of Wriggly consistent with the original? How close is the style to that of Grace Nichols?

DAY 5

Big Book 5C pp. 4–7; Pupil's Book p. 69

Shared reading

- Which text focuses mainly on character? What does the other text mainly focus on?
- Which text tells us most about life in a foreign land? Ask the children to justify their answers.

- Make a list of facts about Hindi life the children have learned from studying the text.
- Which text do the children prefer? Why?

Focused word/sentence work

- Identify in the text verbs ending with -*ed* and -*ing*, e.g. wind*ing*, glow*ing*, pierc*ed*, echo*ed*, burst*ing*, end*ed*, gorg*ing*, work*ed*, look*ing*.
- Encourage the children to identify the rules for adding -*ed* or -*ing* to words ending in *e*, and for adding endings to one-syllable verbs with a short vowel, e.g. *hop*, *tip*.

Independent work

- Children investigate spelling rules for verb endings -*ed* and -*ing*.

Plenary

- Revise the spelling rules for adding -*ed* and -*ing*. Ask the children to learn the rules.
- Review the week's work, re-emphasising teaching points and clarifying misconceptions.

Consolidation and extension

- Ask the children to use information books and other reference sources to find out more about Guyana and about Hindi food and festivals.
- Collect prepositions. Assign one word to each child in the class. Ask them to draw a picture illustrating its meaning, together with a sentence using that preposition. Compile the results into a *Book of Prepositions*.
- Copymaster 23 encourages the children to keep a reading journal to record predictions, questions and reflections while reading.
- Encourage the children to use Copymaster 24 to begin a collection of words borrowed from other languages.

Homework

- Page 22 in the Homework Book gives further practice in using prepositions.

Unit 22

Getting Granny's Glasses

Key Learning Objectives

TL1 To investigate a range of texts from different cultures, considering patterns of relationships, social customs, attitudes and beliefs

TL2 To identify the point of view from which a story is told and how this affects the reader's response

TL3 To change point of view, e.g. tell an incident or describe a situation from the point of view of another character or perspective

TL7 To write from another character's point of view, e.g. telling an incident in letter form

TL10 To write discursively about a novel or story, e.g. to describe, explain, or comment on it

SL5 To revise use of apostrophes for possession (from Y4 term 1)

WL5 To investigate and learn spelling rules: words ending in *e* drop *e* when adding *-ing*; words ending in modifying *e* keep *e* when adding a suffix

WL7 To recognise the spelling and meaning of the prefixes *in-, im-, il-, ir-*

WL12 To use dictionaries efficiently to explore spellings, meanings, derivations

Range:	Novels and stories from a variety of cultures and traditions
Texts:	From *Getting Granny's Glasses*, Ruskin Bond
Resources:	Big Book 5C pp. 8–12 Pupil's Book 5 pp. 70–72 Homework Book 5 p. 23: Prefixes: *in-, im-, il-* and *ir-*

DAY 1

Big Book 5C pp. 8–10; Pupil's Book pp. 70–71

Shared reading

- What is the setting of the story? Which clues tell us?
- From whose point of view is the story told? How does this affect the reader's response?
- Discuss Granny's problem. Why is getting to the eye hospital not easy? What does Granny say about her eyes? What are her real feelings about her eyesight?

Focused word/sentence work

- Identify polysyllabic words with unstressed vowels, e.g. "presence", "hospital", "particular", "capable". Ask the children to learn the spellings.
- Identify the word "blackberry" in the text. What is its plural? Investigate the spelling rule for adding a suffix to words ending in *y* preceded by a consonant.

Independent work

- Children answer questions on the text.

Plenary

- Review the children's independent text work. Discuss the children's opinions about Granny.

DAY 2

Big Book 5C pp. 8–10; Pupil's Book p. 71

Shared reading

- What do Mani and his father think about Granny and her glasses? Do the children think she will be persuaded to go to the eye hospital? What makes them think so?
- How might new glasses change Granny's life?
- Ask the children to read the text aloud, using punctuation to help their reading.

Focused word/sentence work

- Identify words in the text with a modifying (or "magic") *e*, e.g. *pine, hate*. Ask the children to suggest other words with a modifying *e*. Investigate which can be changed by adding suffixes other than *-ing*, e.g. hate*ful*, hope*less*, love*ly*. Write down the spelling of these words and then ask the children to work out the spelling rule for themselves.
- Ask them to learn the spelling rule.
- Investigate the prefixes *in-, im-, il-* and *ir-*. What effect do they have on the meaning of words?

Independent work

- Children investigate and learn the spelling rule for adding suffixes to words ending in a modifying *e*.
- Children recognise and use the prefixes *in-, im-, il-* and *ir-*.

Plenary

- Review the children's independent work. Ensure that the children understand the spelling rule for adding suffixes to words ending in a modifying *e*, and the effect of adding the suffixes *in-, im-, il-* and *ir-* to a word.

DAY 3

Big Book 5C pp. 8–10; Pupil's Book p. 72

Shared reading and writing

- What kind of person do the children think Granny is? Encourage them to justify their responses by referring to the text.
- Plan discursive writing about her, using the structure suggested in the Pupil's Book. Brainstorm ideas. Organise these ideas into paragraphs.

Focused word/sentence work

- Investigate the use of commas, semi-colons and colons in the text. What is the function of each?

Independent work

- Children write discursively about Granny in the story *Getting Granny's Glasses*.

Plenary

- Discuss the children's discursive writing. Exchange ideas about Granny.

DAY 4

Big Book 5C pp. 11–12; Pupil's Book p. 72

Shared reading

- Is this outcome what the children expected? Why?

- Why was the doctor horrified at Granny's glasses? Refer the children to the earlier extract, describing the condition of her glasses, if they are not sure. In what way might her glasses have done more harm than good?

- Why, at first, could Granny not see the eye test board? What do you think the doctor did to make her see clearly?

- What does the last paragraph tell us about the doctor? What does it tell us about Granny?

Focused word/sentence work

- Ask the children to identify prepositions in the text, e.g. *in, out, with*. Point out that prepositions can be compound, e.g. *in front of, apart from, because of, due to.*

- Ask the children to use these prepositions in sentences of their own.

Independent work

- Children write a letter in the role of Granny's grandson, Mani, giving his point of view of events.

Plenary

- Ask the children to read their letters aloud. Discuss the change of viewpoint.

DAY 5

Big Book 5C pp. 11–12; Pupil's Book p. 72

Shared reading

- Read the text again.

- How might Granny react when she can see Mani, his father and her friends clearly? Keeping in mind how she spoke to the doctor, what do the children think she might say?

- Do the children know anyone like Granny? In what way(s) are they similar?

Focused word/sentence work

- Revise the use of the apostrophe for possession, e.g. *Granny's glasses, Granny's eyes*. What are the rules for using the apostrophe? The easiest way to remember this is that the apostrophe always goes immediately after the owner, e.g. *Granny's glasses: Granny*, the apostrophe and then the *s*. This rule applies equally with plural owners, e.g. *the men's coats: the men*, the apostrophe and then the *s*. If the word is plural and ends in *s* there is no need for a second *s*, e.g. *the boys' shoes*. With a name ending in *s*, e.g. *Mr Jones's car*, we usually add an *s*.

Independent work

- Children revise the use of the apostrophe for possession.

Plenary

- Review the week's work, re-emphasising teaching points and clarifying misconceptions.

Consolidation and extension

- Ask the children to collect from their reading examples of: words with the suffixes *in-, im-, il-* and *ir-*; suffixes added to words ending with a modifying *e*; uses of the apostrophe to denote possession.

- If children have difficulty remembering the rule for the use of the apostrophe to denote possession, ask them to underline the owner and then add the apostrophe and the *s*.

- Teaching the correct use of the apostrophe often results in a rash of incorrect apostrophes for plural nouns. Wherever this occurs, encourage the children to ask themselves why they have used an apostrophe. Does it show that someone owns something? Does it show that a word, or words, have been shortened? If the answer is "no" to both questions, no apostrophe is required.

Homework

- Page 23 in the Homework Book consolidates recognising the spelling and meaning of the prefixes *in-, im-, il-* and *ir-*. This activity also gives practice in defining words, and in using a dictionary to explore spellings and meanings.

Unit 23 — The Banana Machine

Key Learning Objectives

TL1	To investigate a range of texts from different cultures, considering patterns of relationships, social customs, attitudes and beliefs
TL2	To identify the point of view from which a story is told and how this affects the reader's response
TL3	To change point of view, e.g. tell an incident or describe a situation from the point of view of another character or perspective
TL7	To write from another character's point of view, e.g. telling an incident in letter form
TL9	To write in the style of the author
SL4	To use punctuation marks accurately in complex sentences
SL6	To investigate clauses through: identifying the main clause in a long sentence; understanding how clauses are connected
SL7	To use connectives to link clauses within sentences

Range:	Novels, stories from a variety of cultures and traditions
Texts:	From *The Banana Machine*, Alexander McCall Smith
Resources:	Big Book 5C pp. 13–16 Pupil's Book 5 pp. 73–75 Homework Book 5 p. 24: Clauses

Preparation

- Make an atlas or gazetteer available on day 1 for the children to locate Port Antonio in Jamaica.

DAY 1

Big Book 5C pp. 13–14; Pupil's Book pp. 73–74

Shared reading

- What clues are there that the story is set in a distant land? Which clue can be used to find out exactly where? (Port Antonio). How might the children use this clue? (atlas, index or gazetteer).
- How did Grandfather Michael lose the plantation? What effect did this have?
- What kind of man do the children think Grandfather Michael was? What makes them think so?

Focused word/sentence work

- The word "banana" is a word borrowed via Spanish or Portuguese from the native name for the fruit in Guinea. Investigate the origins of other words for foods, e.g. *orange* (from the Spanish word *naranja*); *lemon* from the French *limon* (now "lime"); *spaghetti, lasagne, pizza* from Italian (*pasta* is Italian for "paste"); *curry* from the Tamil *kari*, meaning "sauce".

Independent work

- Children answer questions on the text.

Plenary

- Review the children's independent text work. Discuss what they thought about Grandfather Michael gambling away the plantation, and his neighbour taking it from him.

DAY 2

Big Book 5C pp. 13–14; Pupil's Book p. 74

Shared reading

- How did the plantation pass to Aunt Bat? Ask the children to explain the problem facing the family. How would the children in the class feel if they were in that situation?
- What course of action is Aunt Bat planning if the worst comes to the worst?
- Do the children think Aunt Bat is very likely to lose the farm? Would she have told the children if it were unlikely? Why is she telling them now?
- What do they think will happen next?

Focused word/sentence work

- Investigate clauses in sentences. Most sentences have a main clause with one or more subordinate clauses:

  "Because the plantation was so small, *Aunt Bat did most of the work*."

  The main clause (*Aunt Bat did most of the work*) makes complete sense on its own, but the subordinate clause (*because the plantation was so small*) does not.
- Note the use of commas to separate clauses within sentences.

Independent work

- Children identify the main clause in two-clause sentences, and add a main clause of their own to subordinate clauses.

Plenary

- Review the children's independent work on main clauses, re-emphasising teaching points and clarifying misconceptions.

DAY 3

Big Book 5C pp. 13–14; Pupil's Book p. 75

Shared reading and writing

- Is the story told from a single viewpoint? What makes the children think so?
- Encourage the children to put themselves in Patty's place. What does she think about their situation? What clues are there in the text? What effect might this have on her? Is there anything she can do to help? (e.g. work harder, be sympathetic and understanding to her aunt).
- Plan together a letter from Patty to a friend, explaining their predicament and expressing her thoughts and feelings.

Focused word/sentence work

- Investigate the spelling of unstressed vowels in polysyllabic words, e.g. neigh*bours*, af*terwards*, pock*et*.

Independent work

- Children imagine they are Patty in the story and write a letter about the family's situation from her point of view.

Plenary

- Review the children's letters. What different perspectives do the letters have on events?

DAY 4

Big Book 5C pp. 15–16; Pupil's Book p. 75

Shared reading

- Is this how the children expected the story to continue? Discuss similarities and differences between the story and what the children expected.
- What might happen next? What clue is there in the title of the book from which this extract comes, *The Banana Machine*? What kind of machine might change their fortunes? How might they get such a machine?
- Brainstorm ideas, and plan a continuation of the story.
- Write the first paragraph in the style of the author.

Focused word/sentence work

- Investigate the spelling of unstressed vowels in polysyllabic words, e.g. *particularly*, prop*erly*, mo*ment*, dam*age*, cou*sin*, mer*chant*, di*sa*ppoin*ted*.
- Ask the children to identify prepositions in the text, e.g. *over, out, until, down, up, on*.

Independent work

- Children continue the story in the style of the author. This activity will need further time outside the literacy hour.

Plenary

- Review the work in progress. Encourage the children to edit and revise their work.

DAY 5

Big Book 5C pp. 15–16; Pupil's Book p. 75

Shared reading

- Why was Aunt Bat delighted, yet at the same time sad, with Patty's work?
- What new things do we learn about Patty and Mike from this part of the story?
- What facts about banana growing can we learn from this extract?

Focused word/sentence work

- Investigate clauses in sentences. Ask the children to identify the main clause in selected sentences.
- Discuss the difference between a phrase and a clause. (A clause includes a verb.)

Independent work

- Children explore joining sentences to make a complex sentence with main and subordinate clauses.

Plenary

- Review the week's work on clauses, re-emphasising teaching points and clarifying misconceptions.

Consolidation and extension

- Ask the children to substitute new subordinate clauses in the sentences in sections A and B (day 2)on page 74 in the Pupil's Book, without changing the main clause.
- Ask the children to identify main clauses in sentences from their reading.
- Encourage the children to use information books and IT sources to find out more about banana plantations.

Homework

- Page 24 in the Homework Book consolidates work on clauses.

Unit 24

Akimbo and the Crocodile Man

Key Learning Objectives

TL1	To investigate a range of texts from different cultures, considering patterns of relationships, social customs, attitudes and beliefs
TL2	To identify the point of view from which a story is told and how this affects the reader's response
TL3	To change point of view, e.g. tell an incident or describe a situation from the point of view of another character or perspective
TL9	To write in the style of the author
SL4	To use punctuation marks accurately in complex sentences
SL6	To investigate clauses through understanding how clauses are connected (by combining three short sentences into one)
SL7	To use connectives to link clauses within sentences
WL5	To investigate and learn the spelling rule: *i* before *e* except after *c* when the sound is *ee*; note and learn exceptions
WL11	To use a range of dictionaries and understand their purposes
WL12	To use dictionaries efficiently to explore spellings and meanings
WL13	To compile own class/group dictionary using personally written definitions

Range:	Novels, stories from a variety of cultures and traditions
Texts:	From *Akimbo and the Crocodile Man*, Alexander McCall Smith
Resources:	Big Book 5C pp. 17–20 Pupil's Book 5 pp. 76–78 Homework Book 5 p. 25: Using a dictionary

Preparation

- Make a dictionary available for day 5, preferably *Collins School Dictionary*. Note that this particular dictionary will be useful later in helping the children investigate derivations.

DAY 1

Big Book 5C pp. 17–19; Pupil's Book pp. 76–77

Shared reading

- What clues are there that this story is set in Africa?
- What relationship is Akimbo to John? What clues are there that Akimbo has been on the river with John before?
- Why have they landed on the island? How can the children tell?
- From whose point of view is the story told? Ask the children to justify their answers. If the story were told from John's point of view, how would it change?

Focused word/sentence work

- What is a "cicada"? Note its soft *c*.
- Discuss the spelling rule: *i* before *e* except after *c* when the sound is *ee*, e.g. *receive*. Make a list of such words, including exceptions, e.g. *species*.

Independent work

- Children answer questions on the text.

Plenary

- Review the children's independent text work. Discuss the children's ideas on what might have happened to John.

DAY 2

Big Book 5C pp. 17–19; Pupil's Book p. 77

Shared reading

- Ask the children to explain in their own words what Akimbo did, and what John was doing before he found himself in trouble.
- In what ways was the island dangerous? How might someone as experienced as John have got himself into trouble? Was he wise to leave Akimbo alone?
- What would the children have done if they were (a) John; (b) Akimbo?

Focused word/sentence work

- Use examples in the Pupil's Book to investigate how three short sentences may be combined into one. Ask the children to identify the main clause.

Independent work

- Children combine three short sentences into one.

Plenary

- Review the children's independent work. Discuss the children's use of commas. Identify the main clause in each sentence.

DAY 3

Big Book 5C pp. 17–19; Pupil's Book p. 78

Shared reading and writing

- Discuss what might have happened to John. What might Akimbo do to help?
- Plan a new chapter of the story in the style of the author. Brainstorm ideas for four paragraphs, explaining what happens when Akimbo finds John, how he rescues him, gets him safely off the island, and how it all ends.
- Write the first paragraph together in the style of the author.

Focused word/sentence work

- Investigate the variety of sentence constructions used by the author.

Independent work

- Children write a new chapter in the style of the author, resolving the predicament of the characters.

Plenary

- Review the work in progress, offering help and encouragement.

DAY 4

Big Book 5C p. 20; Pupil's Book p. 78

Shared reading

- Is this how the children expected the story to continue? What might the "dark shape" be? What other clues are there to what has happened to John?
- What danger is Akimbo in as he rescues John? How does he drive away the crocodile?
- Why was it important for John to pull himself out of the water? Is he now safe? What makes the children think so?

Focused word/sentence work

- Investigate the connectives used to link clauses in the longer sentences. Which sentences have more than two clauses?
- Ask the children to identify main and subordinate clauses.

Independent work

- Children continue writing their new chapter.

Plenary

- Review the children's writing. Encourage them to edit and review their work. Allow time outside the literacy hour for the children to complete their work.

DAY 5

Big Book 5C p. 20; Pupil's Book p. 78

Shared reading

- Ask the children to tell the incident from John's point of view, using clues and evidence in the text.
- What might happen next? How badly hurt might John be? How will they get off the island to safety?
- Ask the children to retell both parts of the story in the role of either Akimbo or John.

Focused word/sentence work

- Discuss how a dictionary might be used to check spellings and meanings.
- Revise alphabetical order.
- Select words from the text for the children to suggest definitions for, and for them to check these with a dictionary, preferably *Collins School Dictionary*.

Independent work

- Children use dictionaries to explore spellings and meanings.

Plenary

- Review the children's dictionary work.
- Give further practice in checking on spellings and meanings.
- Encourage the children to keep their own class/group dictionaries using personally written definitions of technical words, words connected with a current topic etc.

Consolidation and extension

- Encourage the children to read *Akimbo and the Crocodile Man* to find out what happened to Akimbo and John.
- Introduce the children to a wider range of dictionaries: phrases and idioms (e.g. *Brewer's Dictionary of Phrase and Fable*), slang, rhyming, contemporary usage, synonyms, antonyms, quotations, and a thesaurus. Discuss their different uses and how they help readers and writers.
- Encourage the children to use information books or IT sources to find out more about crocodiles.

Homework

- Page 25 in the Homework Book gives further practice in using dictionaries to explore spellings and meanings.

Unit 25   In My Opinion

Key Learning Objectives

TL12 To read and evaluate letters intended to protest, complain, persuade, considering (i) how they are set out, (ii) how language is used, e.g. to gain attention, respect, to manipulate

TL13 To read newspaper comment, headlines, adverts; compare writing which informs and persuades, considering the deliberate use of ambiguity, half-truth, bias and how opinion can be disguised to seem like fact

TL14 To select and evaluate a range of texts, in print and other media, for persuasiveness, clarity, quality of information

TL15 From reading, to collect and investigate use of persuasive devices

TL17 To draft and write individual, group or class letters for real purposes

WL12 To use dictionaries efficiently to explore abbreviations

Range:	Persuasive writing to put or argue a point of view: letters, commentaries, to persuade, criticise, protest, object, complain Dictionaries
Texts:	Newspaper cuttings: reports, headlines, opinion poll results, letter, advertisement From *Young Letter Writers*, letters chosen by the Royal Mail
Resources:	Big Book 5C pp. 21–25 Pupil's Book 5 pp. 79–81 Homework Book 5 p. 26: Abbreviations Copymaster 25: Persuasive words and phrases

Preparation

- Make available a dictionary with a list of common abbreviations and their meanings, preferably *Collins Junior Dictionary*.

- Collect suitable examples of persuasive writing for the children to investigate outside the literacy hour.

DAY 1

Big Book 5C pp. 21–23; Pupil's Book pp. 79–80

Shared reading

- Is the report about school uniforms fair? Does it truthfully report the children's opinions? Whose opinion does the report really express?

- Read the three different headlines for the same opinion poll results. Are they all true? What different impressions do they give? Why do the children think different newspapers have given a different slant to the results?

- What is the main message in the letter from a "disgusted pensioner"?

- Why is the Koldban advertisement made to seem like a news report? Are readers likely to approach a news report differently from an advertisement? Why?

Focused word/sentence work

- Investigate the range of persuasive devices the "disgusted pensioner" has used. These may be recorded on Copymaster 25.

Independent work

- Children answer questions on the text.

Plenary

- Review the children's answers to the comprehension. Discuss the advertisement for Koldban. Is it really the amazing breakthrough it claims to be? What makes the children think so?

DAY 2

Big Book 5C pp. 21–23; Pupil's Book p. 80

Shared reading, including focused word/sentence work

- Investigate the use of bias and half-truths in the report on school uniforms. Read the actual words of the children who were asked about the wearing of school uniform, and then the newspaper report. How has the reporter twisted their words? Why has he done this?

- Discuss the difference between fact and opinion. Investigate how Koldban has disguised opinion as fact. Is it a fact that Koldban is a breakthrough? Who says it is? Do the manufacturers really believe this, or is it something they would like the reader to believe?

- What effect do the words "amazing" and "revolutionary" have? Try deleting them. Discuss the effect of the changes. Why is Koldban said to be "probably the best cold remedy in the world"? What effect does "probably" have?

- What have "laboratory tests" really proved? Might cold symptoms go within 48 hours even without Koldban? And what about that phrase "in most cases"? What effect does it have?

- Imagine someone has complained to Bennet and Crawford that taking Koldban did not clear up their cold in 48 hours. Ask the children to pick out words and phrases from the advertisement which the manufacturers could use in their defence, e.g. "will, *in most cases*, banish symptoms". They might also ask whether the cold sufferer took the remedy at the very first sign of a cold. If he woke up with his cold, the first symptoms would have shown up while he was asleep, meaning he failed to take Koldban at the right time!

Independent work

- Children investigate the use of persuasive devices in the news report on school uniforms and the Koldban advertisement.

Plenary

- Compare the children's factual versions of the news report and the advertisement with the original. Re-emphasise the difference between fact and opinion.

DAY 3

Big Book 5C pp. 24–25; Pupil's Book p. 81

Shared reading and writing, including focused word/sentence work

- Read the letter *Dear BBC*. What is the writer's point of view? What arguments support it? What does he want the BBC to do?
- Choose a topic for a real letter to a newspaper, perhaps a topical issue. Discuss it with the children, noting different points of view. Encourage the children to explain why they think the way they do, and what they would like to see done.
- Plan a sample letter with a real audience in mind. Who will read the letter? Is it for the editor, the readers of the paper, or both? Show how the ideas and opinions can be organised into paragraphs.
- Discuss appropriate ways of opening and closing the letter.
- Tell the children that they will develop their own letter over two or more drafts.

Independent work

- Children plan and write a first draft of a letter to a newspaper.

Plenary

- Ask the children to read aloud their first drafts for evaluation. Encourage an atmosphere of constructive criticism.

DAY 4

Big Book 5C pp. 24–25; Pupil's Book p. 81

Shared reading

- Discuss the first drafts of the children's letters. Explore how they have presented their arguments. Is everything clear? Is everything organised properly into paragraphs? Might the opening and closing be improved?
- Have the children used any persuasive devices? Are there too many, as in the letter from the "disgusted pensioner"? What effect do the children's persuasive devices have?
- Compare the letters with *Dear BBC*.

Focused word/sentence work

- Investigate punctuation in the letter to the BBC. Note the use of commas in lists, to separate clauses, and in the greeting and closing of the letter.
- Revise the use of the apostrophe. Ask the children to identify examples of its use to show possession, and in contractions. Note the use of the apostrophe with singular and plural nouns, e.g. *adults' programmes*, *nature's example*. Remind the children that the apostrophe comes immediately after the owner, whether singular or plural.

Independent work

- Children edit their first drafts and present their work in a finished state.

Plenary

- Ask the children to read aloud their finished letters. Include finished examples of at least one letter which has shown improvement since the first draft.

DAY 5

Big Book 5C pp. 21–25; Pupil's Book p. 81

Shared reading

- How does the writer of the letter to the BBC gain attention? What persuasive devices does he use? Are his questions genuine or rhetorical?
- What do the children think of his arguments? To what extent do they agree or disagree with him?
- Compare his letter with the one from the "disgusted pensioner". Which is the most clearly reasoned? Why? Which one contains the most persuasive devices? Does this make it more persuasive? Ask the children to justify their answers.
- Identify and classify the persuasive devices in the "disgusted pensioner's" letter.

Focused word/sentence work

- What does "BBC" stand for? Provide the children with dictionaries, such as *Collins Junior Dictionary*, which have a list of common abbreviations. Explore the abbreviations. Classify them into those which stand for a single word, a number of words, and those for organisations and countries.
- What is the difference in meaning between *pm* and *PM*? Or *p* and *P* (pence and parking)?

Independent work

- Children explore abbreviations, using a dictionary, preferably *Collins Junior Dictionary*.

Plenary

- Review the range of persuasive devices explored during the week. Ask the children to collect further examples from their reading, recording and classifying them on Copymaster 25.

Consolidation and extension

- Send the children's letters to a newspaper.
- Copymaster 25 encourages the children to collect, from their reading, examples of persuasive words and phrases and to classify them.
- Use Copymaster 25 to identify and classify the persuasive devices used in the news cuttings in the Big Book.
- Ask the children to look for persuasive devices in TV and radio advertisements. Discuss how tone of voice, music and images can work as persuasion devices. Record suitable adverts for group discussion.
- Make a class or group dictionary of common abbreviations.

Homework

- Page 26 in the Homework Book explores abbreviations.

Unit 26 Riches of the Rainforest

Key Learning Objectives

TL14 To select and evaluate a range of texts, in print and other media, for persuasiveness, clarity, quality of information

TL15 From reading, to collect and investigate use of persuasive devices

TL16 Note-making: to fillet passages for relevant information and present ideas which are effectively grouped and linked

TL19 To construct an argument in note form or full text to persuade others of a point of view and present the case to the class or a group; evaluate its effectiveness

SL2 To understand how writing can be adapted for different audiences and purposes

WL4 To spell unstressed vowels in polysyllabic words

WL13 To compile own class/group dictionary using personally written definitions of technical terms

Range:	Persuasive writing to put or argue a point of view
Texts:	From *The Blue Peter Green Book*, Lewis Bronze, Nick Heathcote and Peter Brown From *Earth Alert*, James Marsh
Resources:	Big Book 5C pp. 26–29 Pupil's Book 5 pp. 82–84 Homework Book 5 p. 27: Changing sentences

Preparation

- Make available books, magazines and newspaper articles about the rainforest, for optional reading and discussion both inside and outside the literacy hour.

- Discuss what the children already know about the importance of the rainforests and how they are being destroyed.

DAY 1

Big Book 5C p. 26; Pupil's Book pp. 82–83

Shared reading

- Why does the writer ask the reader to think of Aladdin's cave?

- What is the purpose of this text? What is its message? Which details support this message?

- What effect does the text have on the children? Which words from the text make them feel that way? How successful is the writer in persuading them?

Focused word/sentence work

- Investigate the use of punctuation in the text, e.g. dots, commas. Why are the words "civilized" and "develop" placed inside inverted commas?

- Investigate the spelling of unstressed vowels in polysyllabic words, e.g. trop*ical*, bal*ance*, moun*tain*.

- Note the exception to the rule '*i* before *e* except after *c*': "species".

Independent work

- Children answer questions on the text.

Plenary

- Review the children's independent text work. Discuss the extent to which the destruction of the rainforests is an international disaster.

DAY 2

Big Book 5C pp. 26–28; Pupil's Book p. 83

Shared reading

- Examine the reasons for the destruction of the rainforest. What are the advantages of doing this? Are they really advantages? Might timber, for instance, be obtained from other parts of the world? What are the disadvantages? Does the extinction of a species matter? Might not medicines be obtained elsewhere? Ask the children to balance the two sides. Do they agree with the writer?

- Discuss the clarity and quality of information. If possible, compare this text with similar information you have collected (see preparation above).

Focused word/sentence work

- Experiment with changing nouns into verbs, and vice versa, by adding suffixes, e.g. *destroy – destruction, discover – discovery, provide – provision, develop – development, disappear – disappearance.*

- Discuss the changes that often need to be made to the spelling of the root words before a suffix is added.

- Make a list of suffixes which change verbs to nouns, e.g. *-ion, -ment, -y, ism, -ology, -ance*; and those which change nouns to verbs, e.g. *-ise, -ify, -en.*

Independent work

- Children transform nouns into verbs, and vice versa, by adding suffixes.

Plenary

- Review the children's work on transforming nouns into verbs, and vice versa. Investigate the changes that often need to be made to the spelling of the root words before a suffix is added.

DAY 3

Big Book 5C pp. 26–28; Pupil's Book p. 84

Shared reading and writing, including focused word/sentence work

- Ask the children to study, in small groups, different parts of the text. Select people in turn to summarise the ideas expressed in those parts of the passage.
- Use the headings given in the Pupil's Book to fillet the text for information. Revise how to record this information as notes. Show how to group and link these ideas effectively.

Independent work

- Children make their own notes on the text about the rainforest.

Plenary

- Review the children's notes. Do they include all the relevant details? Are the ideas effectively grouped and linked?

DAY 4

Big Book 5C p. 29; Pupil's Book p. 84

Shared reading

- Compare this text with the earlier one. What new facts does this one contain?
- Ask the children to explain in their own words the impact of logging on the rainforests.

Focused word/sentence work

- Identify the word "shocking" in the first paragraph. What effect does it have? Why has the author used it? Why does he use the word "plundering" instead of "clearing"?
- Discuss the meanings of technical words used in the passage, e.g. "deforestation", "tropical", "logging", "pollutes", "atmosphere". Encourage the children to make their own class/group dictionary of such words with personally written definitions.

Independent work

- Children use their notes to construct an argument in full text to persuade others of a point of view.

Plenary

- Review the children's arguments. Ask the children to prepare to present them to the class on day 5, or outside the literacy hour.

DAY 5

Big Book 5C p. 29; Pupil's Book p. 84

Shared reading

- Investigate the opening sentence. How does it make the reader want to read on? What is the effect of the words "it's a fact"?
- Is the problem of logging confined to the rainforests? Ask the children to refer to the text to justify their answers.
- Ask the children to explain how felling trees causes flooding.
- Compare the information in this text with other information you have collected (see preparation on page 74).

Focused word/sentence work

- Experiment with changing nouns into verbs and vice versa by adding suffixes, e.g. *confine – confinement, clear – clearance, pollute – pollution, created – creation, form – formation, vapour – vaporise, remove – removal, flood – flooding.*
- Discuss the changes that need to be made to the spelling of the root words before a suffix is added.

Independent work

- Children design a poster drawing the attention of the public to the destruction of the rainforest. This will need to be completed outside the literacy hour.

Plenary

- Children present their arguments to the class, or to a group. Evaluate the effectiveness of the arguments.

Consolidation and extension

- Display the children's posters.
- Ask the children to collect further examples of verbs from nouns and nouns from verbs.
- Encourage the children to find out more about the rainforests, using information and IT sources.
- Organise a debate between loggers and conservationists, with the children putting forward, in role, their different points of view.

Homework

- Page 27 in the Homework Book helps the children understand how writing can be adapted for different purposes by changing vocabulary and sentence structures.

Unit 27 Protecting Species

Key Learning Objectives

TL14	To evaluate texts for persuasiveness, clarity, quality of information
TL15	From reading, to collect and investigate use of persuasive devices
TL16	Note-making: to fillet passages for relevant information and present ideas which are effectively grouped and linked
TL18	To write a commentary on an issue on paper or screen, setting out and justifying a personal view; to use structures from reading to set out and link points
WL5	To investigate and learn the spelling rule: words ending in *y* preceded by a consonant change *y* to *ie* when adding a suffix, except for the suffixes *-ly* or *-ing*
WL10	To understand how words can be formed from longer words, e.g. through omission of letters; through omission of prefixes; through the use of acronyms

Range:	Persuasive writing to put a point of view
Texts:	From *The Blue Peter Green Book*, Lewis Bronze, Nick Heathcote and Peter Brown
	From *Protecting Endangered Species*, Felicity Brooks
Resources:	Big Book 5C pp. 30–33
	Pupil's Book 5 pp. 85–87
	Homework Book 5 p. 28: Words from longer words
	Copymaster 26: Finding out

Preparation

- The writing task for this unit is to produce a leaflet informing people about the need to protect whales and dolphins. This activity is planned to take place on days 3, 4 and 5.
- If possible, make available other information sources on whales and dolphins.
- Make available information sources on useful plants, i.e. for food, clothes and medicine. This will enable the children to complete the extension suggestion on page 87 in the Pupil's Book. Copymaster 26 will also help with this activity.

DAY 1

Big Book 5C pp. 30–31; Pupil's Book pp. 85–86

Shared reading

- What is the purpose of this text? How does the writer persuade us of the need to protect these sea creatures?
- What facts does the writer use to support his argument?
- How does he try to persuade the reader to take action?

Focused word/sentence work

- Investigate clauses in the text. Identify the main clause in longer sentences. Note how commas are used to separate clauses.

Independent work

- Children answer questions on the text.

Plenary

- Review the children's independent text work. Discuss why it is wrong to hunt dolphins.

DAY 2

Big Book 5C pp. 30–31; Pupil's Book p. 86

Shared reading

- Why have whales been hunted?
- What change in technology resulted in the existence of whales being threatened?
- Which facts illustrate how the giant blue whale came close to extinction?
- Why do only Japan and Norway hunt whales? Why do you think the word "scientific" has inverted commas around it?

Focused word/sentence work

- Ask the children to identify the word "centuries" in the section about dolphins. Discuss the spelling rule for adding a suffix to words ending in *y* preceded by a consonant. What exceptions are there to this rule? (e.g. the suffixes *-ly* and *-ing*: *shyly*, *frying*).
- Practise adding suffixes to words ending in *y* preceded by a consonant.

Independent work

- Children investigate the spelling rule for adding a suffix to words ending in *y* preceded by a consonant, and revise previously learned spelling rules.

Plenary

- Review the children's independent work. Ensure they understand and can use the spelling rules.

DAY 3

Big Book 5C pp. 30–31; Pupil's Book p. 87

Shared reading and writing, including focused word/sentence work

- Look at how the information is organised. Notice the bullet points in the *Action* section.
- Investigate ways of using this information to produce a leaflet informing people about the need to protect whales and dolphins.
- Plan the format together, using the suggestions in the Pupil's Book.
- Explore the use of headings, numbered lists or bullet points, and italics or underlining to draw attention to important words.
- Encourage the children to suggest suitable slogans.

Independent work

- Children begin work on designing a leaflet informing people about the need to protect whales and dolphins.

Plenary

- Evaluate the children's work. Are their slogans memorable and to the point? Is the leaflet sufficiently well-planned?

DAY 4

Big Book 5C p. 32; Pupil's Book p. 87

Shared reading

- What is the purpose of this text?
- Discuss man's dependence on plants and animals for food, medicine, clothes and other things. Why might the extinction of even one species affect us?
- How is cross-breeding important? Why do we need as many different types of wild plant and animal as possible?

Focused word/sentence work

- Experiment with forming nouns from verbs, e.g. *depend*, *conserve*, *plant*, *clear*.
- Investigate the spelling of unstressed vowels in polysyllabic words, e.g. med*i*cine, fu*tu*re, mo*me*nt, impor*ta*nt.

Independent work

- Children continue work on their leaflets.

Plenary

- Review the children's leaflets. Encourage the children to evaluate and edit their first drafts.

DAY 5

Big Book 5C p. 33; Pupil's Book p. 87

Shared reading

- Why is teosinte so important? Why is it lucky that teosinte survived? How might this fact help persuade people that forests should not be destroyed?
- Make a list of plants used for food, clothes and medicine. Use reference books or IT sources, if necessary.

Focused word/sentence work

- Discuss words formed from longer words: through omission of letters, e.g. *o'clock*; omission of prefixes, e.g. *telephone*; through the use of acronyms, e.g. *radar*.

Independent work

- Children continue work on their leaflets.
- The extension suggestion in the Pupil's Book encourages children to find out about plants used for food, clothes and medicine. Copymaster 26 will help with this.

Plenary

- Evaluate the children's leaflets. If necessary, provide further time outside the literacy hour.

Consolidation and extension

- Design a badge with a slogan for the protection of whales and dolphins.
- Make group or class dictionaries of acronyms or technical words connected with conservation.
- Copymaster 26 helps the children make notes about plants which provide us with food, clothes and medicine, and to record their sources of information.

Homework

- Page 28 in the Homework Book explores words which have been formed from longer words.

Unit 28 Choral Poems

Key Learning Objectives

TL4   To read, rehearse and modify performance of poetry

TL5   To select poetry, justify their choices, e.g. in compiling class anthology

TL11 To use performance poems as models to write and produce poetry in polished forms through revising, redrafting and presentation

WL6   To transform words

WL9   To understand how words vary across dialects

WL13 To compile own class/group dictionary using personally written definitions

Range:	Choral and performance poetry
Texts:	*The Ceremonial Band*, James Reeves
	The Pow-wow Drum, David Campbell
	Rap Connected, Benjamin Zephaniah
Resources:	Big Book 5C pp. 34–39
	Pupil's Book 5 pp. 88–90
	Homework Book 5 p. 29: Slang
	Copymaster 27: Exploring dialect words

Preparation

• The main focus in this unit is performance poems. From day 3 to day 5 the children will work on writing their own performance poem, using those in the book as models. These poems will be reviewed, edited, and evaluated in performance.

DAY I

Big Book 5C pp. 34–37; Pupil's Book pp. 88–89

Shared reading

• Read the two poems aloud.

• What do the children think a *pow-wow* is? What makes them think so?

• What pictures do the poems make in the children's minds? Which poem do the children like best? Why?

• Investigate the rhythm of each poem.

Focused word/sentence work

• Investigate the use of onomatopoeia in *The Ceremonial Band*. Which instruments are best suited to being read by voices that are high, low, loud etc? Experiment with this.

Independent work

• Children answer questions on the text.

Plenary

• Review the children's independent text work. Discuss reasons for the children's preferences.

DAY 2

Big Book 5C pp. 34–37; Pupil's Book p. 89

Shared reading

• Discuss ways the children might perform one of the poems. Which lines are best read by all the children, by smaller groups or by solo voices?

• Rehearse and modify the performance.

Focused word/sentence work

• Revise ways of transforming words, e.g. adding *-er*, *-est*, and *-ing*, changing verbs into the past tense and into nouns by the addition of suitable suffixes.

Independent work

• Children explore transforming a variety of words.

Plenary

• Review the children's independent work, consolidating teaching points and clarifying any misconceptions.

DAY 3

Big Book 5C pp. 34–37; Pupil's Book p. 90

Shared reading and writing

• Discuss ways of performing the second poem.

• Rehearse and modify the performance.

• Discuss how the poems may be used as models for a choral poem of the children's own.

Independent work

• Children plan their own choral poem.

Plenary

• Review children's poems in progress, offering help and encouragement.

DAY 4

Big Book 5C pp. 38–39; Pupil's Book p. 90

Shared reading

• Read *Rap Connected*. In what ways is it similar to the earlier two poems? (e.g. intended to be performed, strong rhythm). How is it different? (e.g. the use of dialect).

• Discuss dialect. How is it different from standard English? When is it appropriate to speak or write in standard English, and when in dialect? Would this poem work as well if it were written in standard English? Ask the children to justify their answers.

Focused word/sentence work

• Make a list of dialect words and phrases which the children use. Ask the children to define them.

• Copymaster 27 will help with this work.

Independent work

- Children continue their choral poems.

Plenary

- Review the children's poems. Experiment with reading some of these aloud. Encourage the children to revise and edit their work.

DAY 5

Big Book 5C pp. 38–39; Pupil's Book p. 90

Shared reading

- Experiment with ways of performing *Rap Connected*. What guide does the poet give his readers? (e.g. bold type, large type).

Focused word/sentence work

- Discuss the differences between dialect and slang.
- Explore rhyming slang.
- Investigate words like "extra", which were once slang words but have now made the transition to standard English. Make sure the children appreciate that the vast majority of slang words quickly fall out of fashion and, like once-fashionable clothes, are seldom used again.
- The words *zoo*, *piano* and *bus* were once slang words. They are also examples of shorter words made from longer words: *zoological gardens*, *pianoforte* and *omnibus*.
- Discuss current slang used by the children.

Independent work

- Children complete their choral poems.
- The extension suggestion encourages the children to explore dialect and slang words.
- Copymaster 27 is designed to help the children to collect and explore dialect words.

Plenary

- Select suitable poems for the class, or groups, to work on in preparation for performance.

Consolidation and extension

- Let the children perform their poems to the class or to other children in the school. Encourage them to evaluate and modify their performances.
- Record the performances on audio or video tape.
- Encourage the class to select other poems suitable for performance, justifying their choices and compiling them into a class anthology.
- Encourage the children to compile their own dialect and slang dictionaries.
- Copymaster 27 is designed to help the children to collect and explore dialect words.
- Discuss differences between words used by children and words used by their elders.

Homework

- Page 29 in the Homework Book explores slang words.

Unit 29   Railway Rhythms

Key Learning Objectives

TL4	To read, rehearse and modify performance of poetry
TL11	To use performance poems as models to write and produce poetry in polished forms through revising, redrafting and presentation
SL5	To revise use of apostrophes

Range:	Choral and performance poetry
Texts:	*Night Mail*, W.H. Auden; *From a Railway Carriage*, Robert Louis Stevenson
Resources:	Big Book 5C pp. 40–43
	Pupil's Book 5 pp. 91–93
	Homework Book 5 p. 30: Proofreading: punctuation and spelling

Preparation

- Note that the children will be working on their own poems on days 3, 4 and 5. This may need to be continued outside the literacy hour.

DAY 1

Big Book 5C pp. 40–41; Pupil's Book pp. 91–92

Shared reading

- *Night Mail* was written to accompany a film about the Royal Mail. Read the poem aloud. Ask the children to listen to its rhythm, and to imagine the pictures the poem describes.
- Discuss how and why the rhythm changes.
- Does the poem have a regular rhyme? What is the rhyming pattern of the verses which do?

Focused word/sentence work

- Investigate the use of punctuation in the poem.
- Identify prepositions, e.g. *at, up, over, from, across, down, towards, in, beside*.

Independent work

- Children answer questions on the text.

Plenary

- Review the children's independent text work. Discuss which lines they like best and why.

DAY 2

Big Book 5C pp. 40–41; Pupil's Book p. 92

Shared reading

- Discuss the use of figurative language, e.g. the train's "snorting", furnaces "like gigantic chessmen".
- Experiment with different ways of reading the poem out loud: as a full group, as smaller groups and as solo voices.
- Modify the performance as appropriate.

Focused word/sentence work

- Revise the use of the apostrophe for possession and contractions. Ask the children to identify and classify examples in the text.

Independent work

- Children revise the use of the apostrophe for possession and contractions.

Plenary

- Review the children's work on the apostrophe, re-emphasising teaching points and clarifying misconceptions.

DAY 3

Big Book 5C pp. 40–41; Pupil's Book p. 93

Shared reading and writing, including focused word/sentence work

- Use *Night Mail* as a model for the children's own performance poem. Brainstorm ideas.
- Plan a shared poem with a different verse for each different part of the journey. Discuss how the rhythm of the poem might change to reflect the progress of the train.
- The poem need not rhyme, but occasional rhyming lines will sound well in performance.

Independent work

- Children plan and begin writing their own performance poem.

Plenary

- Review the children's work on their performance poems, with particular emphasis on how they have captured the rhythm of a train.

DAY 4

Big Book 5C pp. 42–43; Pupil's Book p. 93

Shared reading

- Read R.L. Stevenson's *From a Railway Carriage*. In what ways is it similar to, and different from, *Night Mail*?
- Clap out the rhythm. Is it regular? How does it change?
- Is the rhyme regular? What pattern does it have?
- Which lines do the children like best? Why?
- Which of the two poems do they prefer? Why?

Focused word/sentence work

- Identify examples of similes in the poem, e.g. "as thick as driving rain", "like troops in a battle".
- Investigate the use of punctuation.

Independent work

- Children continue work on their poems.

Plenary

- Ask the children to read parts of their poems aloud. Evaluate how they might be improved.

DAY 5

Big Book 5C pp. 40–43; Pupil's Book p. 93

Shared reading

- Experiment with ways of reading the poem aloud.
- Evaluate and modify the performance.

Focused word/sentence work

- Investigate the use of prepositions in the poem.
- Investigate why both *From a Railway Carriage* and *Night Mail* are written in the present tense. Why is this particularly effective?

Independent work

- Children continue work on their poems.

Plenary

- Ask the children to read their poems aloud. Discuss which lines might be read by the full group, a smaller group or solo voices. Encourage the children to experiment with reading selected lines faster or slower, loudly or more softly, as appropriate.

Consolidation and extension

- Give opportunity for the children to experiment with performing the poem in different ways. If possible, record the performance for evaluation. Encourage them to make any necessary modifications to the performance.
- Let the children perform their poems to another class or to the rest of the school.
- Encourage the children to select other performance poems, building up a repertoire of poems to perform.

Homework

- Page 30 in the Homework Book gives practice in proofreading for punctuation and spelling.

Unit 30   The Borrowers Afield

Key Learning Objectives

TL2	To identify the point of view from which a story is told and how this affects the reader's response
TL3	To change point of view, e.g. tell an incident or describe a situation from the point of view of another character or perspective
TL6	To explore the challenge and appeal of older literature
TL9	To write in the style of the author
SL1	To secure the basic conventions of standard English
SL2	To understand how writing can be adapted for different audiences and purposes
SL4	To use punctuation marks accurately in complex sentences
SL6	To investigate clauses
SL7	To use connectives to link clauses within sentences

Range:	Older literature
Texts:	From *The Borrowers Afield*, Mary Norton
Resources:	Big Book 5C pp. 44–48
	Pupil's Book 5 pp. 94–96
	Homework Book 5 p. 31: Proofreading: standard English
	Homework Book 5 p. 32: Clauses
	Copymaster 28: How am I getting on? – self-assessment
	Copymaster 29: Revision – 1: term 3 assessment master
	Copymaster 30: Revision – 2: Y5 assessment master

DAY I

Big Book 5C pp. 44–46; Pupil's Book pp. 94–95

Shared reading

- From whose point of view is this part of the story being told? How can the children tell?
- Do the children think Arietty fully understands the danger the borrowers face? What makes them think so?
- Ask the children to retell the story from Arietty's point of view. What might she think and feel as her father confronts the crow?

Focused word/sentence work

- Investigate the words Pod uses. Why doesn't the author use standard English?
- Identify the features of non-standard English, e.g. double negatives, lack of agreement between verbs and nouns.
- Ask the children to change his words into standard English.

Independent work

- Children answer questions on the text.

Plenary

- Review the children's independent text work. Discuss the children's opinions of Pod.

DAY 2

Big Book 5C pp. 44–46; Pupil's Book p. 95

Shared reading

- Compare this story with adaptations on TV or film of this or other books about the borrowers. How are they similar or different?
- Do the children find the language difficult? Is it more difficult than more recent fiction? Ask them to justify their answers. Is the story easier to listen to than to read? Why?

Focused word/sentence work

- Investigate the complex sentences used in the text. Ask the children to identify the main clause.
- Investigate the use of connectives.

Independent work

- Children consolidate their understanding of clauses.

Plenary

- Review the children's independent work, re-emphasising teaching points and clarifying misconceptions.

DAY 3

Big Book 5C pp. 44–46; Pupil's Book p. 96

Shared reading and writing, including focused word/sentence work

- Brainstorm ideas for writing a new chapter in *The Borrowers Afield* story. What might happen next? How might the incident with the crow change their behaviour? What might they do to protect themselves from similar dangers? What might these dangers be?
- Use the children's ideas to plan a new chapter. Try to end with an exciting incident.
- Investigate the style of the author, e.g. complex sentences, non-standard English for dialogue. Encourage the children to imitate this style in their writing.

Independent work

- Children plan and begin writing a further chapter of the story, in the style of the author.

Plenary

- Review the children's writing. Discuss how effectively they are imitating the style of the author.

DAY 4

Big Book 5C pp. 47–48; Pupil's Book p. 96

Shared reading

- Read the second extract from *The Borrowers Afield*. Why is Homily concerned about entering the old boot? What does this tell us about her character? What does Pod say to reassure her? What does this tell us about Pod?
- How might the borrowers make the boot dry and safe for sleeping in?

Focused word/sentence work

- Identify the features of non-standard English in the dialogue.
- Ask the children to change non-standard English into standard English.

Independent work

- Children continue their writing.

Plenary

- Ask the children to read their chapters aloud. Encourage an atmosphere of constructive criticism.

DAY 5

Big Book 5C pp. 44–48; Pupil's Book p. 96

Shared reading, including focused word/sentence work

- What do the children think "borrowing-bags" are? What things might they contain?
- Ask the children to read the text aloud, with a narrator and two other readers for Pod and Homily. Discuss how punctuation helps the reader.
- Discuss ways of adapting this part of the story for young children of five or six. What things would need to be changed? (e.g. less detail, shorter sentences, words younger children will understand).

Independent work

- Children adapt the first text of *The Borrowers Afield* (on page 94 in the Pupil's Book) for younger children.

Plenary

- Review the children's adaptations of the story.

Consolidation and extension

- Encourage the children to read other books in the *Borrowers* series.
- Give the children the opportunity to read their adaptations of *The Borrowers Afield* to a younger audience.
- At the end of the Copymasters section is a certificate for special achievement in any aspect of English, to be awarded at the teacher's discretion.

Homework

- Page 31 in the Homework Book gives opportunity to secure the basic conventions of standard English by correcting a range of common errors.
- Page 32 in the Homework Book consolidates work on clauses.

ASSESSMENT

- Copymaster 28 is a self-assessment sheet for the children to record the aspects of language they enjoy or find easy, and those they would like more help with. The completed sheet will be useful to the children's next teacher.
- Copymasters 29 and 30 are assessment masters of key word and sentence objectives.
- Copymaster 29 covers key objectives for term 3, testing the children's ability to: use prepositions correctly; form antonyms with a suitable prefix; combine three short sentences into one; use abbreviations in context.
- Copymaster 30 revises key objectives for the year, testing the children's ability to: change direct speech into reported speech; distinguish between homophones; use relative pronouns correctly; secure the basic conventions of standard English by correcting a range of common errors.
- Indirectly, both Copymasters will also test vocabulary, spelling and handwriting. The completed sheet will be useful as a record of progress, together with examples of the pupil's text work.

Copymasters

Name _____

Copymaster 1
Unit 1

Story openings

The way a story opens is important in making the reader want to read on. Some stories begin with a description of the setting or of the main character. Others begin with action or dialogue.

Title _____ **Author** _____

How does this story begin?

_____

_____

Do you think this is a good opening? What makes you think so?

_____

_____

_____

_____

_____

Compare this opening with that of another story you have read, perhaps by the same author.

How are they similar or different?

_____

_____

_____

_____

_____

Focus on Literacy Teacher's Resource Book 5 © Barry and Anita Scholes, HarperCollins*Publishers* Ltd 1999

Name _____

Investigating character

Title _____ **Author** _____

Main character _____

Is this story written in the first or the third person? _____

How is the main character introduced? By description, action or dialogue?

_____

_____

How does he or she behave?

_____

_____

_____

_____

_____

How does he or she get on with other characters in the book?

_____

_____

_____

_____

_____

What do you think about this character?

_____

_____

_____

_____

**Copymaster 3
Unit 1**

Reading log

Make notes of your ideas and impressions as you read a book.

Title _____

Author _____

The opening

How does the book open? Is it a good opening? Do you think you are going to enjoy the book? What makes you think so?

_____

_____

_____

_____

_____

Half way through the book

Is the book what you expected? Are you enjoying it? Give reasons for your answers.

How do you think the book will end? What makes you think so?

_____

_____

_____

_____

_____

After you have finished the book

What did you think about the book? Would you recommend it to a friend? Give a reason for your answer.

_____

_____

_____

_____

Focus on Literacy Teacher's Resource Book 5 © Barry and Anita Scholes, HarperCollins*Publishers* Ltd 1999

Copymaster 4 Unit 2

Book review

Star rating guide

★ ★ ★ ★ ★   a great read!

★ ★ ★ ★   a very good read

★ ★ ★   a good read

★ ★   not such a good read

★   a disappointing read

Title _____

Author _____

Publisher _____

Star rating:

How did the story open?

_____

_____

_____

Write words or phrases which you think make the opening especially interesting.

_____

_____

_____

Write words from the text which introduce the main character.

_____

_____

_____

What is your opinion of him or her?

_____

_____

_____

How did the book make you feel?
Which particular events made you feel that way?

_____

_____

_____

Copymaster 5
Unit 2

How stories are structured

Use this sheet to investigate how stories are structured.

Title _____ **Author** _____

Pace
Does the story move slowly or swiftly from one interesting event to the next?
Give an example.

_____

_____

_____

Build-up
How does the story build up towards the most interesting parts?
Give an example.

_____

_____

_____

_____

Complication
Explain the problems the main character faces.

_____

_____

_____

_____

Resolution
How does the main character overcome these problems?
How does the story end?

_____

_____

_____

_____

Focus on Literacy Teacher's Resource Book 5 © Barry and Anita Scholes, HarperCollins*Publishers* Ltd 1999

Copymaster 6
Unit 2

Collecting everyday expressions

Use this sheet to collect everyday expressions and their meanings.

Everyday expression

beat about the bush

put the cart before the horse

bite the dust

Meaning

approach something in a roundabout way

start at the wrong end

fall to the ground

_____   _____

_____   _____

_____   _____

_____   _____

_____   _____

_____   _____

_____   _____

_____   _____

_____   _____

_____   _____

_____   _____

_____   _____

_____   _____

_____   _____

_____   _____

Comparing poems by the same author

When you have read a number of poems by the same author you will begin to notice similarities in subject matter and style (the way the writer uses words). Use this sheet to help you look for similarities.

Poet _____

Poems I have read by this poet:

_____

_____

_____

How are they similar in subject?

_____

_____

_____

_____

_____

_____

_____

How are they similar in style?

_____

_____

_____

_____

_____

_____

_____

Focus on Literacy Teacher's Resource Book 5 © Barry and Anita Scholes, HarperCollins*Publishers* Ltd 1999

Glossary of language terms

This glossary lists explanations of specialist words used in studying English. The words in **bold** in the explanations are also in the main glossary list.

adjective — An adjective describes a **noun**.
a blue bus, a heavy box, interesting books

adverb — An adverb tells us more about a **verb**.
He blows the trumpet loudly. She drives carefully.

alliteration — Alliteration is using several words together which begin with the same sound.
Hannah hurried home happily.

antonym — An antonym is a word with an opposite meaning to another.
hot – cold, wet – dry, light – dark

apostrophe (') — An apostrophe is a **punctuation mark** like a raised **comma**. It is used for short forms of words, showing that one or more letters have been missed out.
I'm = I am, don't = do not
It is also used to show that something belongs to someone.
Elizabeth's mother, Carl's coat

colon (:) — A colon is a **punctuation mark** used to introduce a list.
He bought many things from the market: food, shoes, books and a clock.

comma (,) — A comma is a **punctuation mark** used to separate words in a list.
She wore an old, threadbare, woolly, red coat.
He took a drink, sandwiches, biscuits and a slice of cake.
A raised comma is known as an **apostrophe**.

consonant — A consonant is any letter which is *not a* **vowel**. The vowels are *a, e, i, o, u.*

simile — A simile compares one thing to another. Similes contain the words *like* or *as*. See also **metaphor**.
as quick as lightning   as slow as a snail

singular — Singular is the form of a word which refers to just one person or thing.
apple, potato, baby, wolf, goes, does, waits, listens

speech marks — Spoken words in stories are put inside speech marks.
"What kind of dog is that?" asked David.
Speech marks are also known as inverted commas.

standard English — Standard English is the most common form of English used in writing. It uses standard forms of words and follows rules on spelling, sentence structure and **punctuation.**

suffix — A suffix is a group of letters which is added to the end of a root word to make a new word. Some common suffixes are *-ful, -fully, -ness, -less, -able.*
hope + ful = hopeful   comfort + able = comfortable

synonym — Words with similar meanings are called synonyms. Synonyms can be found in a **thesaurus.**
small, tiny, minute, microscopic, teeny

tense — Verb tense is the form of the **verb** which tells us when something happens, in the past, present or future.
present tense: *he walks, he is walking*
past tense: *he walked, he was walking*
future tense: *he will walk, he will be walking*

thesaurus — A thesaurus is a book that has lists of words which have similar meaning. We use a thesaurus to help us choose more interesting words.

verb — A verb is an action word.
He writes.   She jumped.   They ran.   The dog barked.

vowel — The vowels are *a, e, i, o, u.* Sometimes *y* acts as a vowel, e.g. in *spy.*

person	A text may be written in: the first person (*I said …, I am …*) the second person (*you said …*) or the third person (*she said …, they are …*)
plural	Plural means more than one. *apples, potatoes, babies, wolves.*
prefix	A prefix is a group of letters added to the beginning of a word to make a new word. Some common prefixes are *un-, mis-, in-, im-, dis-, pre-, re-.* *un + tidy = untidy dis + approve = disapprove*
pronoun	A pronoun is a word that stands for a **noun**. Jo is clever. *She* is clever. The cat scratched Ian. *It* scratched *him*.
proofreading	Proofreading means checking of a piece of written work carefully.
punctuation	Punctuation refers to marks such as **commas**, full stops, **question marks**, **exclamation marks**, **colons** and **apostrophes**.
question mark (?)	A question mark comes at the end of a question. *What is your name?*
reported speech	Reported speech tells what people said without using their actual words. There are no **speech marks** in reported speech. In reported speech the present **tense** changes to the past **tense**. *I* and we change to *he, she* or *they*, unless you are talking about yourself. Direct speech: *"I'm too tired to do any more," said Jake.* Reported speech: *Jake said that he was too tired to do any more.*
rhyme	Words that rhyme sound very similar, especially at the end. *cat, mat; bin, thin; sun, run; fuss, discuss; reading, leading*
rhythm	Rhythm is a regular beat in poetry or music.

dialogue	Dialogue in a book, a play or a film is a conversation.
direct speech	Direct speech is the actual words of a speaker. **Speech marks** are placed around the spoken words. *"I'm going to London in the morning," said Jody.*
exclamation	An exclamation is a sentence which gives a command, warning or threat. It is also used to show surprise. *Stop! What a beautiful picture!* An exclamation ends with an **exclamation mark**.
exclamation mark (!)	An exclamation mark is used at the end of an **exclamation**.
homophone	A homophone is a word with the same sound as another word but a different spelling. Homophones are often confused. *write/right; to/too/two; their/there; hear/here*
metaphor	A metaphor is an unusual and effective way of describing something. A **simile** says something is *like* something else. A metaphor says something *is* something else. *My feet were blocks of ice. He is a tower of strength.*
noun	A noun is a naming word. Proper nouns are the special names of people and places, spelt with capital letters. *Louise, Paul, Glasgow, France, Essex* Nouns that are not proper nouns are called common nouns. *book, window, car, rabbit, pencil* A collective noun names a collection of living things or objects. *a flock of sheep, a class of school children, a string of beads*
onomatopoeia	Onomatopoeia is when a word or phrase imitates the sound of the thing it names, e.g. *crash, bang, hiss.*
paragraph	A paragraph is a number of sentences (one or more) about the same subject. A new paragraph begins on a new line, and slightly in from the side of the page.

Copymaster 10
Unit 4

How a story develops

All stories have high and low points. Some start with an exciting event. Others build to an exciting event in the second or third chapter. Most books have an exciting final chapter.

Use this sheet to help you map out the structure of a story book.

Title _____ **Author** _____

High points (What happens in the most exciting chapters?)

_____

_____

_____

Low points

_____

_____

_____

Plot profile

Shade in this plot profile to show the high and low points of the book.

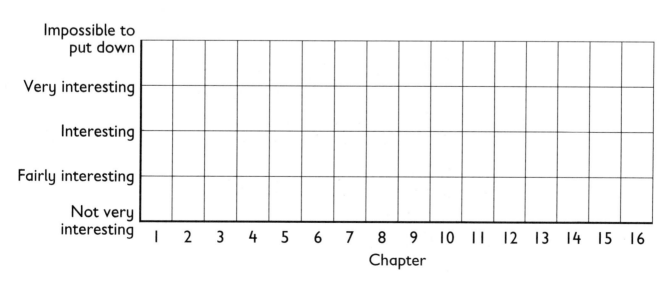

Anne Frank's Diary

Imagine you are Anne Frank. Continue her diary from where the extracts left off.

To think about

How will the family cope with Father's illness?

Can they trust anyone from outside to help them?

Will the family have more mysterious rings at the doorbell?

Will anyone break in looking for hidden bicycles?

Will the door disguised as a bookcase be discovered?

What other events might Anne report?

Focus on Literacy Teacher's Resource Book 5 © Barry and Anita Scholes, HarperCollins*Publishers* Ltd 1999

Story board

Copymaster 12
Unit 8

Title _____

Author _____

1	**2**	**3**
Notes/word bank	Notes/word bank	Notes/word bank

4	**5**	**6**
Notes/word bank	Notes/word bank	Notes/word bank

Books with lasting appeal

Some books have been favourites with generations of children.
Choose one such book that you have read and enjoyed.

Title _____ **Author** _____

Date first published _____

Why I enjoyed this book (think about its plot, characters and setting).

_____

_____

_____

_____

Why adults enjoyed this book. (Talk to an adult who has enjoyed this book. Ask them why
they liked it.)

_____

_____

_____

_____

Why I think this book has lasting appeal (compare your own comments with those of your
adult reader).

_____

_____

_____

_____

Focus on Literacy Teacher's Resource Book 5 © Barry and Anita Scholes, HarperCollins*Publishers* Ltd 1999

Copymaster 14
Unit 10

Revision – term 1 assessment master

1. Add speech marks and any other necessary punctuation to these sentences.

   a) Where is that music coming from asked Fee

   b) I think theres a band in the market place replied Annette lets go and find out

   _____

   _____

2. Change these direct speech sentences to reported speech.

   a) "I have been to see Aunty Jane," said Jonathan.

   b) "Why is there no football game on Saturday?" asked Abu.

   _____

   _____

3. Change these present tense sentences to past tense.

   a) He is going to the park, but his friends are painting.

   b) I am mowing the grass while my friend clips the hedge.

   _____

   _____

4. Change these sentences to the future tense.

   a) I went to the match on Saturday.

   b) She is taking her dog to the vet.

   _____

   _____

5. Use these words and phrases in sentences of your own.

   a) upset

   b) under the weather

   c) sign

   d) as strong as a horse

   _____

   _____

   _____

Different versions of the same story

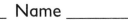

You can often find more than one version of the same traditional story.
Use this sheet to compare them.

Version 1 (title, author, etc.) _____

Version 2 _____

What is the basic story they both tell?

_____

_____

_____

_____

_____

_____

In what ways are the versions different?

_____

_____

_____

_____

_____

_____

Suggest reasons for these differences.

_____

_____

_____

_____

_____

_____

Focus on Literacy Teacher's Resource Book 5 © Barry and Anita Scholes, HarperCollins*Publishers* Ltd 1999

**Copymaster 16
Unit 14**

Finding out: planning sheet

When looking for information, use this sheet to help plan your search.

Lots!

What do I know already?

_____

_____

_____

_____

_____

Lots more!

What do I want to find out?

_____

_____

_____

_____

_____

????

How can I find out?

_____

_____

_____

_____

_____

????

Where can I find this information?

_____

_____

_____

_____

_____

Name _____

Copymaster 17
Unit 14

Finding out: finding and recording information

Write your question here.
Underline the <u>key words</u>

My question:

_____

_____

Choose two suitable books from the library.

Write their titles, and then your key words below.

Look up your key words in the books' indexes. Write their page number(s).

1st book title: _____

1st key word	_____ page number(s)	_____
2nd key word	_____ page number(s)	_____
3rd key word	_____ page number(s)	_____

2nd book title: _____

1st key word	_____ page number(s)	_____
2nd key word	_____ page number(s)	_____
3rd key word	_____ page number(s)	_____

Scan for the information you need. Write the answer to your question:

_____

_____

_____

_____

Focus on Literacy Teacher's Resource Book 5 © Barry and Anita Scholes, HarperCollins*Publishers* Ltd 1999

**Copymaster 18
Unit 16**

Exploring genre

Genre refers to different types of story, e.g. legends and folk tales, science fiction, historical stories, adventure etc. Each genre has its own characteristics. When you have read a few stories in one genre, use this sheet to make notes on its characteristics.

Genre:
What kind of story are you writing about? _____

Settings: (time and place)
What settings do these stories usually have?

_____

_____

_____

Characters:
What kinds of character appear in these stories?

_____

_____

_____

Objects:
Do special objects appear in these stories, e.g. magic swords?

_____

_____

_____

Plot:
What kinds of thing happen in these stories?

_____

_____

_____

Language:
How is the language different from other types of story?
Do these stories have unusual words, e.g. technical words, old-fashioned words etc?

_____

_____

_____

Name _____

Copymaster 19
Unit 17

A glossary of terms

Technical words are the special words used frequently in some subjects, but uncommon in everyday English. For example, computer science uses words such as *byte*, *hard disk* and *RAM* (random access memory).

Use this sheet to collect technical words and their definitions.

Technical word	**Definition**
_____	_____
_____	_____
_____	_____
_____	_____
_____	_____
_____	_____
_____	_____
_____	_____
_____	_____
_____	_____
_____	_____
_____	_____
_____	_____
_____	_____
_____	_____
_____	_____
_____	_____

Focus on Literacy Teacher's Resource Book 5 © Barry and Anita Scholes, HarperCollins*Publishers* Ltd 1999

Copymaster 20
Unit 17

Comparing information texts

Some information books and IT sources are more useful than others. Choose two texts on a subject you are researching and compare them.

Text 1

Title _____

Author _____ **Publisher** _____

Text 2

Title _____

Author _____ **Publisher** _____

Which text had the best contents or index? _____

Which had the best headings? _____

Which was the easiest to understand? Why? _____

_____

_____

_____

Which text was most useful? Why? _____

_____

_____

_____

Which had the best illustrations? Why? _____

_____

_____

_____

Rate the texts on a scale of 1 to 5, with 5 as the best.

	Index/contents	Easy to read	Information	Illustrations	Overall
Text 1	_____	_____	_____	_____	_____
Text 2	_____	_____	_____	_____	_____

Focus on Literacy Teacher's Resource Book 5 © Barry and Anita Scholes, HarperCollins*Publishers* Ltd 1999

Name _____

Book review

Title _____ **Author** _____

Who is telling the story, the author or one of the characters? _____

Who is the hero or heroine of the story? _____

Who is the villain? _____

How does the author make you feel about these characters?

_____

_____

_____

_____

_____

_____

_____

Write about an exciting part of the story. From whose point of view is it told?

_____

_____

_____

_____

Write about a part of the story told from the point of view of a different character.

_____

_____

_____

_____

_____

Focus on Literacy Teacher's Resource Book 5 © Barry and Anita Scholes, HarperCollins*Publishers* Ltd 1999

Name _____

Revision – term 2 assessment master

1. Use each word in a sentence of your own to show its meaning.

   a) waist _____

   b) waste _____

   c) scene _____

   d) seen _____

2. Join these sentences in a suitable way. Do not use "and".

   a) She finished painting the cupboards. She sat down to rest.

   _____

   b) I met a man. He used to live in Central Africa.

   _____

   c) I found the ring. I lost it last year.

   _____

3. Put each of these clauses in a sentence of your own.

   a) but did not stop to look

   b) which was cracked and chipped

   c) because it was raining in

   d) when the phone rang

   _____

   _____

   _____

   _____

4. Complete each sentence with a suitable clause of your own.

   a) He dropped the box _____

   b) She went for a walk _____

   c) This is the lady _____

   d) It was half past two _____

Name _____

Reading journal

Keep a reading journal. As you read a book, write down what you think about the story and its characters, the questions you would like the book to answer, and how you think the story might end.

Title _____ **Author** _____

What do you think of this book?

_____

_____

_____

_____

What do you think of the main character? What do you think he or she should do next? Why?

_____

_____

_____

_____

What questions would you like this story to answer?

_____

_____

_____

_____

How do you think the story might end?

_____

_____

_____

Focus on Literacy Teacher's Resource Book 5 © Barry and Anita Scholes, HarperCollins*Publishers* Ltd 1999

Words borrowed from other languages

Collect words which have been borrowed from other languages.

Word	Definition	Origin
veranda	a roofed terrace at the front or side of a building	Hindi

Focus on Literacy Teacher's Resource Book 5 © Barry and Anita Scholes, HarperCollins*Publishers* Ltd 1999

Copymaster 25
Unit 25

Persuasive words and phrases

Collect persuasive words and phrases from your reading. You will find them in newspapers and magazines (especially letter columns), advertisements, circulars etc.

Sort them under these headings.

Words and phrases

e.g. "surely"; "it wouldn't be very difficult ..."

_____

_____

_____

_____

_____

Persuasive definitions

e.g. "the real truth is ..." (Is it the real truth, or what the writer would like us to believe?)

_____

_____

_____

_____

_____

Agreeing with part of the opposite point of view

e.g. "Naturally, we can't expect the problem to be solved overnight ..."
(This makes the writer's argument seem reasoned and balanced.)

_____

_____

_____

_____

_____

Questions which are not true questions, but statements (rhetorical questions)

e.g. "Are we expected to ...?" (The writer really means: "We are not expected to ...")

_____

_____

_____

_____

_____

Deliberate ambiguities

e.g. "the professionals' choice" (Do <u>all</u> professionals choose this? Or just two or three?)

_____

_____

_____

_____

_____

Focus on Literacy Teacher's Resource Book 5 © Barry and Anita Scholes, HarperCollins*Publishers* Ltd 1999

Copymaster 26
Unit 27

Finding out

Use this sheet to make notes about plants which
provide us with food, clothes and medicine.

Food
_____
_____
_____
_____
_____

Clothes
_____
_____
_____
_____
_____

Medicine
_____
_____
_____
_____
_____

I found these books and/or other information sources useful in my research:

_____
_____
_____

Focus on Literacy Teacher's Resource Book 5 © Barry and Anita Scholes, HarperCollins*Publishers* Ltd 1999

Exploring dialect words

Copymaster 27
Unit 28

Find out the words people use for these things in your dialect.
Choose more words of your own to explore.

Words to ask about	Children	Adults	Grandparents
hello			
goodbye			
good			
bad			
nothing			
money			
snack			
plimsoll			

Focus on Literacy Teacher's Resource Book 5 © Barry and Anita Scholes, HarperCollins*Publishers* Ltd 1999

How am I getting on? – self-assessment

Tick the things you enjoy or find easy (or draw a smiley face next to them).
Put a cross against the things you would like more help with.

Speaking, talking and listening

talking about stories or poems

reading aloud by myself

reading aloud with others

Writing

stories

longer stories

playscripts

poems

writing about books

letters

reports

non-chronological reports

explanations

instructions

making notes

presenting a point of view

punctuation

spelling

standard English

Reading

stories and novels

traditional stories

poems

plays

reports

letters

instructions

information books

using a contents page and index

using a dictionary

persuasive writing

IT sources

Copymaster 29
Unit 30

Revision – 1: term 3 assessment master

Name _____

1. Complete these sentences with a suitable preposition.

a) He stood _____ the bridge, looking _____ at the canal _____ him.

b) The canal went _____ the bridge, _____ the hill and _____ a tunnel.

2. Change these words to their opposites by adding a suitable prefix. Write your own definition for the word you have made.

a) expensive _____

b) legal _____

c) possible _____

d) patient _____

3. Combine each set of three sentences into one.

a) This is Mr Smith. He is wearing a grey suit. He is carrying a briefcase.

_____

b) The forecast is correct. We will have a blizzard. The road will be blocked.

_____

c) After the burglary he was worried. He bought a dog. The dog was fierce.

_____

d) You go out. Go to the shops. Buy me some bread.

_____

4. Use each abbreviation in a sentence of your own to show its meaning.

a) DJ _____

b) am _____

c) UFO _____

d) ITV _____

114

Focus on Literacy Teacher's Resource Book 5 © Barry and Anita Scholes, HarperCollins*Publishers* Ltd 1999

Copymaster 30
Unit 30

Revision – 2:
Y5 assessment master

1. Change these direct speech sentences to reported speech.

  a) "I'm late," she said. _____

  b) "Where is John going?" he asked. _____

  c) "Take care," she warned them. _____

2. Use each homophone in a sentence of your own.

  a) (there) _____

  b) (their) _____

  c) (write) _____

  d) (right) _____

  e) (hear) _____

  f) (here) _____

3. Complete these sentences with *who, whose* or *which*.

  a) This is the fierce dog _____ chased off the robbers.

  b) Bill, _____ is in my class at school, has
     just come back from a holiday in Canada.

  c) Mrs Morris, _____ daughter won the race,
     is very pleased.

4. Write each sentence correctly.

  a) Nina and me is the best of friends.

  _____

  b) I'm not going nowhere if my friends isn't going too.

  _____

  c) Everybody were pleased when the results was read out.

  _____

  d) We done us best to help him, but he don't say a word of thanks.

  _____

Focus on Literacy 5
Achievement Award

Awarded to _____

For _____

Signed _____   Date _____

School _____

Focus on Literacy 5
Achievement Award

Awarded to _____

For _____

Signed _____   Date _____

School _____

Focus on Literacy Teacher's Resource Book 5 © Barry and Anita Scholes, HarperCollins*Publishers* Ltd 1999

RECORD SHEET

NAME _____   CLASS _____

Year 5 • Term 1

Word level work: phonics, spelling, vocabulary

Objective	Comment
Spelling strategies	
1 Identifying own misspelt words	
2 Using known spellings to spell other words	
3 Using independent strategies	
Spelling conventions and rules	
4 Properties of words ending in vowels other than *e*	
5 Spelling patterns in pluralisation	
6 Prefixes: *auto, bi, trans, tele, circum*	
Vocabulary extension	
7 Synonyms	
8 Word roots, derivations and spelling patterns	
9 Idiomatic phrases, clichés and expressions	
10 Adverbs to qualify verbs in writing dialogue	

Sentence level work: grammar and punctuation

Objective	Comment
Grammatical awareness	
1 Investigating word order	
2 Basic conventions of standard English	
3 Discussing, proofreading and editing own writing	
4 Adapt writing for different readers and purposes	
5 Difference between direct and reported speech	
Sentence construction and punctuation	
6 Punctuation as an aid to the reader	
7 Dialogue	
8 Verb tense Verb forms: active, interrogative, imperative Person: first, second, third	
9 Imperative form in instructional writing Past tense in recounts	

Text level work: comprehension and composition

Objective	Comment
Fiction and poetry	
Reading comprehension	
1 Analysing and comparing story openings	
2 Comparing structure of different stories	
3 Investigating how characters are presented	
4 How texts can be rooted in the writer's experience	
5 Understanding dramatic conventions	
6 Distinctive style or content of poems by significant poets	
7 Poetic style, use of forms and themes of significant poets	
8 Investigating word play	
9 Developing an active attitude towards reading	
10 Evaluating a book by referring to details and examples in the text	
11 Experimenting with alternative ways of opening a story	
12 Enduring appeal of established authors and "classic" texts	
Writing composition	
13 Recording ideas, reflections and predictions about a book	
14 Mapping out texts showing development and structure	
15 Writing new scenes or characters into a story, in the manner of the writer	
16 Conveying feelings, reflections or moods in a poem	
17 Writing metaphors from original ideas or from similes	
18 Writing own playscript	
19 Annotating a section of playscript for performance	
20 Evaluating script and performance for dramatic interest and impact	
Non-fiction	
Reading comprehension	
21 Identifying features of recounted texts	
22 Evaluating a range of instructional texts	
23 Purpose of note-taking and how this influences the nature of the notes	
Writing composition	
24 Writing recounts based on (a) a close friend and (b) an unknown reader	
25 Writing and testing instructional texts	
26 Making notes for different purposes ·	
27 Using simple abbreviations in note-taking	

Focus on Literacy Teacher's Resource Book 5 © Barry and Anita Scholes, HarperCollins*Publishers* Ltd 1999

NAME _____ CLASS _____

Year 5 • Term 2

Word level work: phonics, spelling, vocabulary

Objective	Comment
Spelling strategies	
1 Identifying misspelt words; learning to spell	
2 Using known spellings to spell words with similar patterns or related meanings	
3 Using independent spelling strategies	
Spelling conventions and rules	
4 Exploring spelling patterns of consonants and formulating rules	
5 Words with common letter strings but different pronunciations	
6 Distinguishing between homophones	
7 Understanding correct use and spelling of possessive pronouns	
8 Recognise and spell the suffix -cian etc.	
Vocabulary extension	
9 Searching for, collecting, defining and spelling technical words	
10 Investigating further antonyms	
11 Exploring onomatopoeia	
12 Investigating common metaphorical expressions and figures of speech	

Sentence level work: grammar and punctuation

Objective	Comment
Grammatical awareness	
1 Re-ordering simple sentences	
2 Consolidating basic conventions of standard English	
3 How writing can be adapted for different audiences and purposes	
4 Revision of the different kinds of noun; function of pronouns; agreement	
Sentence construction and punctuation	
5 Using punctuation effectively in longer and more complex sentences	
6 Awareness of differences between spoken and written language	
7 Exploring ambiguities that arise from sentence contractions	
8 Constructing sentences in different ways, while retaining meaning	
9 Using the comma in embedding clauses within sentences	
10 Using pronouns so that it is clear to what or to whom they refer	

Text level work: comprehension and composition

Objective	Comment
Fiction and poetry	
Reading comprehension	
1 Identifying and classifying features of myths, legends and fables	
2 Investigating different versions of the same story	
3 Similarities and differences between oral and written storytelling	
4 Reading a range of narrative poems	
5 Performing poems in a variety of ways	
6 Terms describing different kinds of poem; identifying typical features	
7 Compiling class anthology of favourite poems with commentaries	
8 Distinguishing between author and narrator	
9 Investigating different fiction genres	
10 Differences between literal and figurative language	
Writing composition	
11 Own versions of legends, myths and fables	
12 Writing extensions based on poems read	
13 Reviewing and editing	
Non-fiction	
14 Making notes of story outline as preparation for oral storytelling	
15 Investigating and noting features of a range of explanatory texts	
16 Preparing for reading by identifying what they already know	
17 Locating information confidently and efficiently	
18 Knowing how authors record and acknowledge their sources	
19 Comparing how different sources treat the same information	
20 Note-making	
Writing composition	
21 Converting personal notes into notes for others to read	
22 Planning, composing, editing and refining non-chronological reports and explanatory texts	
23 Recording and acknowledging sources in their own writing	
24 Evaluating own work	

Focus on Literacy Teacher's Resource Book 5 © Barry and Anita Scholes, HarperCollins*Publishers* Ltd 1999

NAME _____   CLASS _____

Year 5 • Term 3

Word level work: phonics, spelling, vocabulary

Objective	Comment
Spelling strategies	
1 Identifying misspelt words; learning to spell	
2 Using known spellings to spell words with similar patterns or related meanings	
3 Using independent spelling strategies	
Spelling conventions and rules	
4 Spelling unstressed vowels in polysyllabic words	
5 Investigating and learning spelling rules	
6 Transforming words	
7 Recognising the spelling and meaning of prefixes	
Vocabulary extension	
8 Everyday words borrowed from other languages	
9 Understanding how words vary across dialects	
10 Understanding how words can be formed from longer words	
11 Using a range of dictionaries and understanding their purposes	
12 Using dictionaries efficiently to explore spellings, meanings, derivations	
13 Compiling own class/group dictionary using personally written definitions	

Sentence level work: grammar and punctuation

Objective	Comment
Grammatical awareness	
1 Securing the basic conventions of standard English	
2 How writing can be adapted for different audiences and purposes	
3 Prepositions	
Sentence construction and punctuation	
4 Using punctuation marks accurately in complex sentences	
5 Using apostrophes for possession	
6 Investigating clauses	
7 Using connectives to link clauses and sentences	

Text level work: comprehension and composition

Objective	Comment
Fiction and poetry	
Reading comprehension	
1 Investigating a range of texts from different cultures	
2 Identifying the point of view from which a story is told	
3 Changing point of view in a story	
4 Reading, rehearsing and modifying performance of poetry	
5 Selecting poetry, justifying choices	
6 Exploring the challenge and appeal of older literature	
Writing composition	
7 Writing from another character's point of view	
8 Recording predictions, questions, reflections while reading	
9 Writing in the style of the author	
10 Writing discursively about a novel or story	
11 Writing and producing performance poems	
Non-fiction	
Reading comprehension	
12 Letters to inform, protest, complain, persuade	
13 Comparing writing which informs and persuades	
14 Evaluating texts for persuasiveness, clarity, quality of information	
15 Collecting and investigating use of persuasive devices	
16 Note-making	
Writing comprehension	
17 Individual, group or class letters for real purposes	
18 Writing a commentary on an issue	
19 Constructing an argument	

Focus on Literacy Teacher's Resource Book 5 © Barry and Anita Scholes, HarperCollins*Publishers* Ltd 1999

Appendices

NLS and *Focus on Literacy*: overview charts

Term I

Word level	Sentence level	Text level
1 Continuous work	1 Unit 9	1 Units 1, 2, 5, 9
2 Continuous work	2 Continuous work; Units 1, 8	2 Unit 2
3 Continuous work	3 Continuous work; Units 2, 7	3 Units 1, 5, 8, 9
4 Unit 2	4 Unit 8	4 Units 1, 6, 8
5 Units 2, 3	5 Units 1, 3	5 Units 4, 5
6 Unit 5	6 Continuous work; Units 8, 9, 10	6 Unit 3
7 Units 4, 10	7 Units 1, 4	7 Units 3, 10
8 Unit 6	8 Continuous work; Units 5, 7, 8	8 Units 2, 3, 5
9 Unit 2	9 Unit 7	9 Units 1, 2, 6, 8
10 Unit 4		10 Units 1, 2
		11 Unit 9
		12 Units 1, 2, 4, 9
		13 Unit 1
		14 Unit 4
		15 Units 1, 2
		16 Units 3, 10
		17 Units 10
		18 Units 4, 5
		19 Units 4, 5
		20 Units 4, 5
		21 Unit 6
		22 Unit 7
		23 Units 7, 8
		24 Unit 6
		25 Unit 7
		26 Units 6, 7, 8
		27 Units 7, 8

Term 2

Word level	Sentence level	Text level
1 Continuous work	1 Units 16, 17	1 Units 11, 12, 13, 14, 15, 16
2 Continuous work	2 Continuous work; Unit 19	2 Units 12, 20
3 Continuous work	3 Unit 12	3 Units 12, 13, 20
4 Units 11, 15, 17	4 Units 13, 14, 15	4 Units 18, 19
5 Unit 18	5 Units 17, 20	5 Units 18, 19
6 Unit 12	6 Units 12, 13	6 Unit 18
7 Unit 15	7 Units 13, 19	7 Unit 18
8 Unit 19	8 Units 12, 16, 17	8 Units 13, 20
9 Unit 17	9 Units 15, 17, 20	9 Unit 16
10 Units 16, 18	10 Unit 13	10 Units 12, 16, 18, 19
11 Unit 11		11 Units 11, 12, 15, 16, 20
12 Units 16, 20		12 Units 18, 19
		13 Units 12, 15, 16, 20
		14 Unit 13
		15 Unit 17
		16 Unit 17
		17 Unit 17
		18 Unit 17
		19 Unit 17
		20 Units 14, 17
		21 Unit 14
		22 Units 14, 17
		23 Unit 17
		24 Units 12, 14, 16, 17, 20

Term 3

Word level	Sentence level	Text level
1 Continuous work	1 Continuous work; Unit 30	1 Units 21, 22, 23, 24
2 Continuous work	2 Units 26, 30	2 Units 21, 22, 23, 24, 30
3 Continuous work	3 Unit 21	3 Units 22, 23, 24, 30
4 Units 21, 26	4 Units 23, 24, 30	4 Units 28, 29
5 Units 21, 22, 24, 27	5 Units 22, 29	5 Unit 28
6 Units 21, 28	6 Units 23, 24, 30	6 Unit 30
7 Unit 22	7 Units 23, 24, 30	7 Units 22, 23
8 Unit 21		8 Unit 21
9 Unit 28		9 Units 21, 23, 24, 30
10 Unit 27		10 Unit 22
11 Unit 24		11 Units 28, 29
12 Units 22, 24, 25		12 Unit 25
13 Units 24, 26, 28		13 Unit 25
		14 Units 25, 26, 27
		15 Units 25, 26, 27
		16 Units 26, 27
		17 Unit 25
		18 Unit 27
		19 Unit 26

Medium frequency words to be taught through Years 4 and 5

Teachers should expect many Y4 pupils to have little or no difficulty reading most of the words below. However, they may have difficulties in spelling them accurately. Many of these words do not follow a regular pattern and others are easily confused. The list is intended as a check for spelling. It is not intended that teachers should go slavishly through the lists, teaching by drilling, though there is an important place for practice, reinforcement and testing. There are many ways in which these words can be investigated and learned e.g. through grouping them by meanings, common spelling patterns, sound patterns, locating them in dictionaries and other texts, creating mnemonics, inventing and playing word games, proof-reading and checking them in independent writing. The words are grouped for ease of teaching. A complete list is provided overleaf should teachers wish to regroup them to suit the needs of their classes.

Year 4 Term 1

ask(ed), began, being, brought, can't, change, coming, didn't, does, don't, found, goes, gone, heard, I'm, jumped, knew, know, leave, might, opened, show, started, stopped, think, thought, told, tries, turn(ed), used, walk(ed)(ing), watch, write, woke(n)

Year 4 Term 2

almost, always, any, before, better, during, every, first, half, morning, much, never, number, often, only, second, sometimes, still, suddenly, today, until, upon, while, year, young

Year 4 Term 3

above, across, along, also, around, below, between, both, different, following, high, inside, near, other, outside, place, right, round, such, through, together, under, where, without

Year 5 Term 1

baby, balloon, birthday, brother, children, clothes, garden, great, happy, head, heard, something, sure, swimming, those, word, work, world

Year 5 Term 2

earth, eyes, father, friends, important, lady, light, money, mother, own, paper, sister, small, sound, white, whole, why, window

Year 5 Term 3

Use this term to check up on spelling knowledge from previous terms

Years 4 and 5

above
across
almost
along
also
always
animals
any
around
asked
baby
balloon
before
began
being
below
better
between
birthday
both
brother
brought
can't
change
children
clothes
coming
didn't
different
does
don't
during
earth
every
eyes
father
first
follow(ing)
found
friends

garden
goes
gone
great
half
happy
head
heard
high
I'm
important
inside
jumped
knew
know
lady
leave
light
might
money
morning
mother
much
near
never
number
often
only
opened
other
outside
own
paper
place
right
round
second
show
sister
small

something
sometimes
sound
started
still
stopped
such
suddenly
sure
swimming
think
those
thought
through
today
together
told
tries
turn(ed)
under
until
upon
used
walk(ed)(ing)
watch
where
while
white
whole
why
window
without
woke(n)
word
work
world
write
year
young